TESTI

Buzz McCarthy is the recognised authority of relationships in Australia. She has an insight never seen before in the field of internet dating and relationships. This brilliant work is a must read for everyone who is single and over 18.

Darren Stephens,

International Speaker & Best Selling Author of 'Millionaires & Billionaires Secrets Revealed'.

Dr McCarthy has written the authoritative book on the subject of internet dating and relationships. This work will no doubt be regarded as the go-to source for people committed to actually finding their true life partner. In time I have no doubt it will be regarded as seminal as Men Are from Mars, Women Are from Venus was for its clarity on modern relationships.

Dr Colbey Forman, Ph.D.,

Dean & President of Beurin University, Founder of the field of Psychoneurology, California, USA

I love this book; it is both timely and authoritative and I am thrilled that someone has finally written on how to successfully navigate internet dating in the 21st century. Dr Buzz McCarthy is a world leader in intimate relationships. Her book is an inspiration and packed full with powerful and real information on relationships.

Vicki Crowe
Founder and CEO, Enneagram Australasia Pty Ltd, Melbourne.

Dr Buzz McCarthy speaks and writes as passionately as she lives. Her workshops are engaging and insightful, with a combination of old and new philosophies entwined to capture the finest of both. Buzz will challenge your perception and beliefs by introducing provocative questions and thinking to drive you to re-think your outlook. Buzz has an amazing focus and determination to achieve her goals which is infectious when she works with other to achieve their goals.

Jodie Cole
Specialist, People and Organisation Development, The Global Fund to Fight AIDS, Tuberculosis and Malaria, Geneva, Switzerland

In the 30 years I have known Dr Buzz McCarthy I have found her to be an outstanding communicator, mentor and teacher. Passionate since her late 20's for self-improvement, she has developed a formidable reputation for positively influencing the lives of others.

Robert Vickers-Willis
Professional Mentoring for Leadership and Team Development, Melbourne

1

Dr Buzz McCarthy is a very gifted person with a powerful yet gentle technique in effectively communicating with people. This book will shine a bright light on the dating world and how to gain real clarity in relationships.

John Hallyburton

Licensed Marriage Celebrant, Melbourne, Australia

Buzz McCarthy is an extraordinary person with an enormous amount of skills and over 30 years' training in personal development which she has incorporated in the many facets of her successful life which include running successful businesses and having a lifestyle that most would envy. Her strength is getting to the source of what a person needs and with her cutting edge technology she creates solutions. She is someone who walks her talk; she has a unique skill set, high standards and an enormous abundance of wisdom. Buzz is a leader and influencer to all those who have the privilege of interacting with her.

Melissa Gilbert, CFP, BA (Econs), Dip FP

Principal, Diamond Financial Solutions Pty Ltd, Sydney, Australia

Buzz has the most uncanny ability to see through the curtain and dive right to the precise place that needs to be exposed. Her intuition is brilliant. The belief she has in her clients and standards she holds them to, insures their certain success.

Cynthia Freeman, MCC, MA.

Executive Coach, Newport Beach, California, USA

INTERNET DATING

Men to Avoid, **Men to Enjoy**

Dr Buzz McCarthy

DISCLAIMER

All the information, techniques, skills and concepts contained within this publication are of the nature of general comment only and are not in any way recommended as individual advice. The intent is to offer a variety of information to provide a wider range of choices now and in the future, recognising that we all have widely diverse circumstances and viewpoints. Should any reader choose to make use of the information contained herein, this is their decision, and the contributors (and their companies), authors and publishers do not assume any responsibilities whatsoever under any condition or circumstances. It is recommended that the reader obtain their own independent advice.

First Edition 2011

Second Edition 2020

McCarthy. Buzz

Internet Dating: Men to Avoid, Men to Enjoy

TO THOSE WOMEN WHO
WILL DO

WHATEVER IT TAKES TO
CREATE A

COMMITTED AND
PASSIONATE

RELATIONSHIP BLENDING
THEIR

VALUES AND STANDARDS
WITH

THEIR LOVING HEARTS.

Dr Buzz McCarthy

ACKNOWLEDGEMENTS

To my clients and colleagues, I would like to thank you for the generosity in allowing me to publish your dating stories: you will know that your truth has been preserved whilst your identities have been changed. Some of you offered your wisdom, your stories and your complete faith in my project, and I thank you for sharing the journey with me, your daily emails of encouragement and your news on the dating front. You have honoured me by taking on board my teachings and you now deserve the man of your dreams!

TABLE OF CONTENTS

INTRODUCTION

CHAPTER 1   First it's about love

CHAPTER 2   Your standards are everything

CHAPTER 3   His job, her job

CHAPTER 4   Internet Dating: What's Good and What's Not

CHAPTER 5   The Relationship Bank Account

CHAPTER 6   Profiles - How to Write Yours and Read His

CHAPTER 7   Navigating through the Dating Maze

CHAPTER 8   Dating on Your Terms

CHAPTER 9   Men to Avoid

CHAPTER 10   Mr Unavailable

CHAPTER 11   Mr Desperate Dan

CHAPTER 12   Mr Sex Only

CHAPTER 13   Mr Cheater

CHAPTER 14   Mr Addict

CHAPTER 15   Mr Remote

CHAPTER 16   Mr Cyber Freak

CHAPTER 17   Mr Blatant Liar

CHAPTER 18   Mr Predator

CHAPTER 19   Is He a Keeper?

CHAPTER 20   Sex: When and When Not

CHAPTER 21   Mr Right

CHAPTER 22   The Final Word

About the Author

INTRODUCTION

In these strange times of Covid-19 Lockdown around the world, internet dating is rampant. People everywhere are seeking to connect with someone; find someone to relate to; seeking ways out of aloneness and loneliness and in the frenzy and presumed urgent-ness are making all the wrong decisions.

Finding a partner is not something you will do well if you are needy. Neediness just manifests neediness and I've always said it's like two people eating from the same plate. Neither is satisfied. Good relationships come from being in the right space in your life to offer something to fill up the other person not simply to take something to fill you up. It's a place where you engage not just your heart, but your head, and you can discern the good from the bad.

In addition, divorce rates are higher than they have been historically, the marriage age is older than ever, there are more single people looking for a mate, and many of them are disillusioned and negative about the dating game: women especially. They tell me how much they want a real relationship and how all the guys they meet want sex, preferably now, without a relationship. And for free.

Whilst there is nothing wrong with that if the women want it too but I'm hearing that most of them don't. They want a committed

10

relationship where they are free to have a family if they wish, have a career and have a partner who loves them exclusively. They think it should be relatively easy yet finding the package seems to be increasingly difficult.

In the past there was the family to introduce you to the nice boy down the road, or you met him at church or other community-based places. Sometimes you met him at work. But life has changed, you wouldn't want the person your family wanted you to meet, you are too busy working to join a heap of clubs and especially now people are working remotely and even without the pandemic we are experiencing, meeting places have changed dramatically. What remains are bars (well not now but normally) which many women think are only pick up places for sex and there is the internet and a proliferation of dating sites where, presumably you can find Mr Right.

But most women can't even find Mr Right Now on the net and they approach it half-heartedly, expecting failure and disappointment. Many are afraid of it, afraid of who is lurking out there. There are too many stories that put them off; stories of predators and of sexual perverts. They don't feel safe; they have one or two setbacks with the guys they meet and they give up.

So they stay at home. Their baby days numbered or their disappointments from a divorce shadow them everywhere. They may do some personal work on themselves and go back to the net with renewed hope but still they can't find a mate to share their lives with.

Their fears are valid. There are some men out there on the net you definitely don't want to get involved with. Lots of them. And there are some great men there too. This book will show you the difference. And it will show you what you need to do to attract the sort of man who will love you forever and commit to a permanent relationship.

CHAPTER ONE

FIRST IT'S ABOUT LOVE

Once upon a time we met the boy next door, drove to the church as a virgin bride and lived happily ever after. We fell in love without really knowing what we wanted, and we settled for what we got. We had kids and a mortgage, we may have worked, we may have had an outside interest or not, the kids grew up and left home and we enjoyed some years with our spouse until one of us left the planet...usually him.

This recipe is certainly not what most women want these days. We want the lot, don't we ladies? - love, passion, commitment, honesty, buckets of money, a beautiful home, travel, maybe a beach house, designer clothes, designer kids and all the gadgets that proliferate in the marketplace.

Who is out there in the marketplace has also changed dramatically with the advent of the internet, no-fault divorce and women earning proper salaries. Not only have the places for finding a mate changed, so have the players and the reasons. The dating game is no longer uniquely for the young; there are plenty of people out there dating from teens to 70's, and beyond and women can and often do take the lead these days.

Also changed is what we want from a committed relationship. Companionship is not enough; we want a relationship of personal satisfaction and deep fulfilment. And we ladies want a man who honours us with his exclusive love, has a career he enjoys, is able to communicate with us about matters of the heart, protect us from the nasties of life and let us have free time to enjoy our girlfriends and the other things we love doing on our own.

That's shouldn't be that hard, should it, in an enlightened society?

But most people, when they enter the arena of the dating ritual, have little idea what they are looking for other than a mate to share their life. They have an outcome - the package - but they don't have a target - who he or she should be for them.

Once upon a time buying a home was the most important decision we made. Now we change homes every few years and if we don't want to change partners with the same regularity then we need to take the blindfold off and get some clarity.

Falling in love does not need intelligence: deciding who you want to spend your life with, does.

Finding someone we are attracted to, allowing a bit of chemistry to kick in and starting the game without knowing what we want is the recipe for the D word......divorce and disaster. Yes, that is what most people go on so the high divorce stats are hardly surprising.

When I ask clients to name the top five things they want in a mate, I often hear "let me think about it for a minute." That's shorthand for I don't have a clue. If they did know, the qualities they wanted would just slip off the tongue naturally.

Some say "great sense of humour, tall, dark and handsome." Yeah, right. But what about including some lasting and desirable qualities like honesty, integrity, confidence and intelligence? Tall dark and etc are great but they're superficial and you can't build a relationship on superficiality.

Neither can you build a sustainable relationship on physical passion; you build a relationship on substantial values, lasting qualities and a joint vision.

The clearer you are about what you want the easier it is to find it, because a part of your brain sorts for what you see as most important. And whether we know it consciously or not, we all have a list.

If you know what is on that list before you enter the arena you are ahead of the game. If you don't know what you want, your relationship could quickly head for the stars with some mutual attraction but if you don't have a few of the jigsaw pieces together other than great sex it may return to earth with a big thud. And you are left wondering what went wrong.

Your destiny is more a matter of choice than chance.

Popular opinion says we can't have it all but I believe we can. Life doesn't need to be a trade off. If we have clarity, focus and determination, and choose our mate wisely and are prepared to do whatever it takes when the going gets tough, we can have it all.

But most of all we need love. It's all about love. I'm not talking about falling in love. That's like a cocaine rush: a rich cocktail of drugs that can herald a roller coaster ride of sleepless nights, loss of appetite, butterflies in the stomach and significantly, loss of rational thought. It's the time when rationality flies out the window and insanity flies in.

Being in love is fun and it's fabulous. We see all the good things and are blind to his faults. We see what we want to see, we try and make him fit into the picture we want and we happily construct a big story of "forever" with a person we barely know. Falling in love is a wonderful time to enjoy and live life to the max; but it is not the time to make life-long decisions.

> **Being in love is all about you getting what you want.**
> **Deciding to love is all about giving him what he wants.**

Long ago, relationships were about an exchange of what was considered valuable. Our maternal ancestors, vulnerable in the wild, needed to nurture their men or there was no food for the family. Women chose their mate on the basis of his ability to protect and provide for her and he went along to meet his needs and to procreate.

Today, not much has changed. Women still want a man to protect and provide, although differently from their forebears and relationships are still about an exchange of what is considered valuable. Women typically want to partner with a man who has access to resources that will enhance her life and research shows she rarely chooses someone who can't match her assets or potential. She wants things like intelligence, financial capacity, faithfulness and commitment. A man wants a partner who will provide him with the things he values. In addition to wanting support, loyalty and faithfulness he wants an unending diet of sex, peace, comfort and more sex, for which he is prepared to share his resources.

In this way, she has what she wants, resources, and he has what he wants, services, and with all the women's liberation in the world, only some of the commodities have changed since tribal days.

18

So where in all this is love? And because this book is a guide for women who want to be in an exclusive and committed relationship, I am talking about conscious loving. This is moving from the heady days of being in love to loving him.....about meeting his needs not just yours, and about doing whatever it takes to be his raving fan.

For starters you have to know that a relationship is a place you go to give. I said "give" not "get". For you to have a love affair with your partner for life you have to love him no matter what. Forget the little things that annoy you, they'll be plenty of stuff about you that annoys him too. It's the small stuff. Get into the big stuff and leave it behind. Get addicted to giving and your life will absolutely change for the best.

Now if this scares you shitless it will be your first hurdle. For love and fear cannot co-exist. If you have fear you cannot love completely. If you have only love there will be no fear. It's a biggie, isn't it? Especially after you've been hurt before; perhaps many times.

But leave those many times behind and get addicted to love if you want the very best love affair of your life....a committed and exclusive relationship that goes on forever.

> **It's not how much we give but how much love we put into giving. Mother Theresa**

Love is a choice. Choosing to love will change everything in your life. It will make you see what is important and what is trivial. It will give you compassion and understanding for those around you and eliminate critical judgement from your life. It is the ultimate privilege given to us. Choose it and create magic for the rest of your life with the love of your life.

NOTE TO SELF:

♥   **My decision is to let go of fear and choose love instead**

♥   **I'm excited about giving at a new level in my relationships**

♥   **I know the top five important things I want in a mate**

CHAPTER TWO

YOUR STANDARDS ARE EVERYTHING

Most women do not know how to date to get what they want. They lose too much of their power and think they have to do everything the guy wants, they have to make arrangements and send texts and emails to get a man to take them out and they have to dress in a way that can make them feel uncomfortably sexy just to attract a man and that they have to be pawed even if they don't want it and feel that if he pays for dinner they have to repay it immediately with sex.

Ladies, all this is rubbish. You don't have to do anything you don't want and you can have all the dates you like, with men whom you'd be happy to introduce to your family, your kids and your friends.

> *It's your standards that will build the foundation for the relationship.*

But it's all up to you. It's your standards that will build the foundation for the relationship. It's your knowing what you want and what you don't want that will enable you to choose the right kind of guy to even have a coffee with and it's your ability to love without fear that will bring a loving man into your life.

21

You don't have to have sex to repay anything. You don't have to kiss him on the first date and you don't have to invite him out to repay a dinner until you want to be in relationship with him. You don't have to text him, you don't have to invite him anywhere, you don't have to arrange anything, that is all his job, and trust me, if you start doing his job, he will not be the man you want.

In fact, one of the reasons you say there are no good men out there is because you have taken over so much of his job that he no longer knows what to do or how to show up.

The fact that you now run companies and countries and have kids at the same time has not made men different. It is you that has changed the scenario, not him. If you want to be ravished by your man, then know that if you run the relationship it won't happen because you will effectively cut off his balls. He needs to do the doing stuff, that's his masculine job so if you want a relationship where you are both in your perfect core energy perhaps it's time to remove your pin-striped suit, find your feminine energy and shine your light for him.

He won't fall in love with you because you are the company president; he will be attracted to your feminine radiance first and will fall in love with you because you are a woman with standards.

To have standards means that you know what you want, go for what you want, don't settle for less and use your standards to grow your feelings of self worth. The bottom line is that men are actually disappointed if you come over - ie give them sex - too soon! I know this will resonate with some of you, many will be relieved, but for those of you who don't get it, please read it again and out loud so you really get it before I explain further. Men are actually disappointed if you come over - ie give them sex - too soon! And this statement comes from men; good men who you would want to have a relationship with and perhaps marry.

Whilst we know that men want sex all the time and preferably on your first date, they actually regard a woman who is a pushover as someone they won't pursue, other than for sex. They are not likely to refuse you, but if they want a good relationship too they are also not likely to pursue you no matter how good you think you are at sex. How good is not the issue, how soon is.

Remember how bad you've felt when you've had sex with someone you've hardly known and you never heard from him again? We've all done it and been dreadfully disappointed by it, haven't we? Well maybe it's news to you, but men are actually disappointed by it too.

They spend their days in the workplace setting goals, marking progress, re-establishing deadlines, working towards an outcome. Sometimes that outcome or that project is years down the track.

Often it is months away. They are totally used to having a long lead time to the finalisation of a project or a deal. That's the sort of things men do for a living, and they are accustomed to it.

When we come over too soon, we are no challenge to them and that actually disappoints them. It takes away their masculine drive. Their masculine energy is all about release, but when it comes too soon they feel flat and sad. Trust me....I have heard this story from too many men to disbelieve it.

Now that doesn't mean they won't take your offer of a roll in the hay on the first date....well some will actually not create the space to do that....but if they do, you are, in their eyes, way too easy. Now if it's the one thing men are afraid of it is their woman going off with someone else and it could well be their greatest fear that if you give them sex too soon you could just as easily have sex with their best friend whilst you are still seeing him.

Don't settle for a relationship that won't let you be yourself.
Oprah Winfrey

So ladies, dating can be on your terms. Know that you can put off sex until you are ready and simply focus on the fun of getting to know new men or joining the dating arena again after a divorce or the end of a long term relationship.

24

It does not need to be frightening or daunting using the internet as a medium for finding men to date. It does not have to be scary. It's up to you to make it safe, fun and successful and it's all about your standards

How you can do that, and the types of men that you should absolutely avoid are all in these pages. Enjoy allowing the man to do his job and whilst you rediscover your feminine energy and do less. Masculine energy is all about doing. You can once more become a human being. The success you will have in the dating game is in direct proportion to the standards you set from day one and the clarity you have about what you want in a relationship and what you are prepared to give.

If you are prepared to give 100% no matter what, your love will be rewarded by love. If you hold back 20% because of fear, your fear will escalate and will be met by fear.

We've all been hurt, that's a given in any relationship and it's not life threatening. This book will give you the confidence to create your own relationship dream around loving no matter what and applying the standards you feel absolutely comfortable with.

There is not only one soul mate for everyone - the universe has a back-up plan, so if at first you don't succeed, move on, quickly and stay in the energy vibration of attraction and love. And whatever you do, have fun and maintain your standards and your essence of feminine power. If enough women do it differently men will get it.

NOTE TO SELF:

♥ **I am very clear about my standards and I will stick to them**

♥ **I will allow him to woo me**

♥ **I totally commit to dating on my terms**

CHAPTER THREE

HIS JOB, HER JOB

Some of the reasons relationships seem to struggle so much these days is the lack of clarity about how we each should show up in the relationship and for each other.

There is still an element of a man's role being to provide and protect and whilst you might think it is something that was only part of your grandparents' lives I believe it's alive and well today. We <u>still</u> want and need our man to provide and protect, although not maybe in the way our ancestors wanted and got. What we need is for him to provide a safety net for our relationship. That's his job. It's like the shell of an egg. We've got to know we feel safe with him to open up and to express ourselves and our love without fear. He has to create that space by his love, by his acceptance of us as we are, by his commitment and his agreement to exclusivity. And if he doesn't do it, then we cannot do our job.

We've got the inside of the egg to be responsible for. That's creating the emotional ambience of the relationship. They're the feminine pieces - like the creation of an atmosphere of romance, of loving, of love-making, of deciding when to have sex the first time, of wanting it to have a loving energy about it and all the gooey stuff. And whilst we know there is an increasing number of men out there who can and want to share this role, it is still primarily the woman's gift to the relationship. It's a bit like

27

creating a beautiful dinner party and inviting your favourite friends in. The emotional ambience of your committed relationship is your job.... getting together all the pieces that make you feel safe and nurtured within the safety net of the shell he has provided. And you can't do it if you don't trust him and respect him.

So you've heard of walking on egg shells, haven't you? Well that happens when the egg cracks so severely that your safety net is full of holes you can fall through or when it's been taken away altogether. You no longer feel secure, you no longer feel protected by your man and you lose either trust or respect, or often both go out the door at the same time. It happens when he threatens the relationship in some way. It certainly happens if he has an affair of the heart; it could be by some addiction like gambling or alcoholism; it happens when he puts significant emotional energy into something or someone other than you. And it happens every time. It's the ultimate betrayal when the egg is broken: the shell lies in pieces on the ground and your safety and your emotional certainty have gone down the plughole. Humpty Dumpty couldn't put it back together again and neither most probably can you.

NOTE TO SELF:

♥ **I will get clarity on his role**

♥ **And I will certainly get clarity on my role**

♥ **I need to decide if I feel safe to love: if not, I will consider the options - do I need to do work on myself or is this the wrong man for me and why**

CHAPTER FOUR

INTERNET DATING: WHAT'S GOOD AND WHAT'S NOT?

The internet is in our lives now whether we like it or not and we can't imagine a life without it. We have access to global resources that our grandmothers and great grandmothers would not ever have thought possible and we can learn amazing stuff without ever leaving home. The resources the internet offers should make our lives easier but they can make our lives more challenging, if we let them.

Having access to potential partners on the internet is a mixed blessing. Granted there is quantity but it takes skills and strategies to make sure that the ones we engage with are quality. The number of women, of all ages, who tell me they haven't had a date in a year or more...sometimes a lot more, is surprising. These women say they want relationships but they have a great story around why it's not happening now, and it's mostly because of fear.

We're not taught how to do relationships right.

We're not taught how to do relationships right. When we play a sport we know the rules before we get onto the field but we don't know how to be in relationships. If we don't practice we will never know what works for us and with the internet offering us so many men we can afford to practice a bit and hope that when "he" comes along we've got it right, or almost right.

In my experience women are too often afraid to ask for what they want in a relationship and yet expect their man to know. If he doesn't she will put him down and bitch to her girlfriends. Whilst the difficult ones will test you to the limit with their power games and their sex games, the nice ones still need your help to understand what you want and how the relationship needs to be for you. It's not that they don't know how to be a great partner but you will be different from their last partner and you need to let them know what you specifically are about. They need to know and understand your standards and your goals and you need to know what you want and be prepared to ask for it; you need to know what you don't want and how to say no when what they want is not right for you, or not right for you right now. And if doing all this is hard face to face, the internet gives you a chance to practice before you meet someone.

What's not good about internet dating is that it can be a breeding ground for people who haven't made it in life and won't make it in the dating arena either. It's much easier for some people to make a computer their best friend instead of having a life, enjoying friendships, joining clubs and going out where they are involved with real people and dating face to face.

> *Women can be picked over by dozens of men and judged by their photograph rather than by their soul.*

Men can "meet" hundreds of women on line and never date one. Women can be picked over by dozens of men and judged by their photograph rather than by their soul. These are some of the downsides of internet dating but whether you like it or not, the internet is here to stay and so is dating via the internet. What you will learn in these pages is how to do it better, for more fun, less heartbreak, less fear, less waste of time and ultimately more success.

NOTE TO SELF:

♥   **I'll research the dating sites that attract me most**

♥   **I'll look at men's profiles and see what they write and what they want**

♥   **I'll look at women's profiles too before I decide what to write for myself**

CHAPTER FIVE

THE RELATIONSHIP BANK ACCOUNT

Ladies, if you really want a loving relationship then you must take your focus off yourself and put it onto him. You must do this no matter what and you must do it without fearing anything. What you need to know from the outset is what you must love and accept is him; every bit of him and all the time.

You always get what you focus on, so if you focus on him leaving, then he probably will. If you really truly want love, then you must focus on love and hold nothing back.

> **Never regret. If it's good, it's wonderful. If it's bad, it's experience.   Victoria Holt**

This is my story of the Relationship Bank Account. Let's say you are not quite sure if your future man is going to hurt you or not, leave you or not or do what the last guy did, whatever that was, which was not nice.

So when you find him, because of the last experience, you make a decision to hold something back and you only put 90 cents in the

Relationship Bank Account. You keep the other 10 cents out "in case." In case he leaves, in case he has sex with someone else, in case he doesn't show up the way you want, in case he does whatever it is you don't like or breaks one of your rules about how a relationship should be, whether it's trivial or whether it's major. In any event because you only put 90 cents in the Relationship Bank Account those 10 cents you kept out become the first 10 cents invested in what I call your exit strategy.

Then, every time things don't go as you want, you'll put another cent or two, or maybe more, in the jar holding your exit strategy. If you have a big argument or disagreement you may find yourself putting a pile of cents in that exit strategy at once or you may just pop a cent or three in from time to time. But because you allow that jar to be close by ready to receive the number of cents in it will creep up on you until one day you'll find it is almost full and there are only a few cents left in the Relationship Bank Account.

Sadly, you'll look at the accumulation of cents in your exit strategy jar, you'll count them, rehash all the reasons that you put them there in the first place and with the newly constructed story that justifies why this man is not for you, you will exercise your exit strategy and you will leave for greener pastures.

If you don't want all your relationships to end this way you will put the full $1 in your Relationship Bank Account and learn to communicate better and resolve challenges when they arise. You will exercise your relationship muscle, you will stick in there and see what is coming up for you to learn and you will grow and finally get the difference between being right and being in this relationship.

So do yourself a favour and choose, if you want to have a lasting and fully loving relationship, to put your full $1 in. And with the energy of that commitment your dollar will accumulate interest not just with your increased love, but with the resolution of those challenges that in the past would have caused you to withdraw yourself, and your cents, from the Relationship Bank Account it will grow even more.

And if you really were not meant to be together you can move on knowing that your ability to love without fear has become the barometer of success of your relationship life.

> **Happiness never decreases by being shared.   Buddha**

NOTE TO SELF:

♥   I will look at my last relationship and work out how much I put in the Relationship Bank Account

♥   I will evaluate why I am not still in that relationship and if it related to how much I gave and how much I held back

♥   I've decided to put in the full $1 next time

CHAPTER SIX

PROFILES - HOW TO WRITE YOURS AND READ HIS

In our teens my friends and I would frock up on a Friday night to meet boys from the neighbouring private schools at a dancing class where our frustrated teacher tried in vain to teach us the Pride of Erin. If we got lucky Simon or Rob or Hughie would invite us down to the Jolly Roger for a milkshake afterwards and hopefully we got invited to the Boatrace Dance and the endless round of School Dances by the boys we met there. Country girls used to do their frocking up during the school holidays when they spent Saturday nights at barn dances in the local church hall. Girls and boys paired up in a circle, the music started, the dancing began and there was just time for a brief chat with each young man before the girls were twirled off to the next one. They progressively moved around the circle until they had done the rounds and the music stopped for a break before the second round. No alcohol, just a lot of fun and a huge network of young people.

The modern day equivalent is speed dating, except that the contenders are plied with champagne and for most there is no second round. Imagine a night of speed dating. You probably don't know anyone other than the friend you went with, drink a nervous glass of champagne or three and spend a few minutes trying to impress a bunch of the opposite sex who talk only about themselves, judge you on how you look, and are probably just as nervous. You end up with an egotistical viewpoint of someone you are not remotely interested in until the formalities end and you can go home to lick your wounds knowing that again you have not encountered your soul mate.

The flow-on effect from the barn dance was the re-connecting of the dancers the following Saturday night or in the next school holidays, providing opportunities to grow friendships and to get to know and appreciate each other's values. The speed dating experience is a one-off. You get just a few minutes to make a very superficial assessment about someone based on a bunch of lies. It would be highly unusual for anyone to ask the question "what do you value most in life" or for someone to know how to answer it if it was asked.

Internet dating seems to have taken the place of family introductions, barn dances, dinner parties and church and for today's time poor people it does seem to have some answers. One great thing about internet dating is that you have the opportunity to get clear about what you want before you start.

When you go on line to create a profile to attract potential partners, you have an opportunity to present yourself in a great light. They don't know you personally, they don't know your friends or your family and they can know only what you put there. The name you choose, the words you write and the photos you display will determine who is attracted to you. Your self-worth, inner strength and standards will determine who you weed out early in the game.

The more confident you are, the easier it is to write the truth about who you are and to easily articulate what you want. Writing your profile also gives you a great opportunity to say up front what you don't want such as a smoker, an atheist, someone with children or a couch potato. You won't scare off anyone who is attracted to your values or your range of interests and you hope it will deter those who are not.

It is vital that your profile reflects something you will bring to the table.

And because relationships are the place to give not to get, it is vital that your profile reflects something you will bring to the table. The men I talk to are sick of women who want stuff from them and whilst most women are happy to share what they have there are still some who expect the man to bring home all the bacon whilst they have their nails manicured or their faces lifted. So creating your profile will determine who you attract, as is the choice of dating sites to join. There is a proliferation of sites blatantly out there for people who want multiple sexual partners and for people who want to cheat on their spouses. I am not talking of them, rather of genuine sites which people join to find a real, lasting and committed relationship.

So if you want a real relationship, your profile must reflect your realness.

Modern women want a man who is masculine enough to go out and earn a good living doing something he is passionate about....in other words to be on purpose, and who is also conscious enough to be able to talk to her on matters of life; and yes we want it all. Many men in their masculine energy can have trouble tapping into their consciousness, their light and their spirit on their own. More often it is found through his woman, or if not, then he can access it through nature, through art and through music. But principally it is through his woman.

So for us to get what we want we have to be what they want - we have to shine a light for them to access the part of them that we deeply desire. This is not something we want to try to be; it is something we must be, naturally and with complete transparency.

This is the giving, nurturing, soft, feminine part of women. It's not the woman in the pin striped three-piece suit stomping the corridors of power in the city each day, going head to head with her male counterparts and wondering why she never finds a bloke in her office to date. It's not the woman who does all the do-do-doing, all the arranging, all the texting, all the organisation. It's not the woman who tells every man she dates that she wants a child because her time clock is ticking away her baby years and it's not the woman who has his income spent before he can tell her what team he goes for.

It's a woman who is in her feminine flow; the one who knows exactly what she wants but allows space and time for things to happen naturally and unhurriedly. It's the woman who knows how loving her heart is and who is waiting for someone to really value and appreciate her before she gives her gifts away. It's the one who is radiant because she is full of love and full of life even without a partner to love. And as you now know he will only fall in love with your radiance, so this is the woman you need to be when you start writing your internet profile and it has to include what you will bring to the relationship, not just what you want.

Unsurprisingly truth is the best way to go; the path of least disappointment and least waste of time. However, there seems to be a general acceptance that a few white lies are OK on your internet profile and given that most people lie a lot in their normal lives, one can certainly appreciate that some embellishments will be included in an on-line profile.

The extent and acceptability of the lies will be revealed in the chapter on Mr Blatant Liar, a little later. But for now, it's up to you to write your profile how you wish to be seen, and the best option is not to be too specific first up. Dating a few men will help you get clearer on what you want so until that happens be general and see what happens. You can always change your profile when you get clarity on something you either can't live with or must have.

Your internet dating pseudonym also tells a story. It's great to have a one-word insight into who you are but don't make it a joke for your audience. Remember the guy's ones you've read that have turned you off: "SexyMate" who is not the least bit sexy, "HomeLover" who wouldn't appeal to a party girl or "RomanticGuy" who turns out to be fat and ugly. Similarly, "LateNightLass" may not appeal to a well brought up Catholic boy who still lives at home and "WantingMySoulMate" is too confronting for most men.

Create an on-line name that you like and that is neither boring nor sexy. If you call yourself something that indicates you are looking for a husband, or something too sexy or serious, men will pass you over or hook into you for sex only. Make your headline fun and avoid a description that is too obvious or over the top. Remember there is a smorgasbord of women out there and you don't want to be passed over because you have a headline that is obscure or too much of a come-on.

Post a photo (or two if you must but no more) that is clear, up to date and shows you smiling. Remember that he will be attracted to your radiance. He won't know or won't care if you are wearing Prada or Gucci just that your eyes smiled at him, so make that happen. Guys are nuclear visual so get a really great photo taken, by a professional if you can, but have it realistic. They complain to me often that women they meet are often 10 years older than their photos (and I know we have the same complaint) but it is very off putting. Be alluring but not sexy, and leave your breasts inside your top. My mother always said it was better to conceal than to reveal; I think she's right, but you don't want to look like

Ms Prude either! Find a balance that presents you the way you want to be seen.

Some clients tell me they don't want to put a photo up because of their career. I think that is irrelevant these days. On-line dating is totally acceptable and you will get far more interest if you have a photo. Men like to see what you look like and you will know from your on-line experience that you will pass over a guy who does not have a picture. Assume they will do the same, even more so!

Photos on men's profiles are also a dead give-away for us ladies and whilst men are pretty visual, we are probably smarter than they think. When we see a blurred photo we take it that they have something to hide, probably their age. If he wears a hat we are forced to think that he is a bit thin on top, which is totally not sexy, whereas fully bald and proud of it is! Men whatever are you thinking having your photo taken beside a sports car? Firstly, we won't believe it's yours, and secondly it indicates that you have nothing of substance but think that an expensive toy will get a good woman hooked. It's a "no" every time, isn't it ladies?? I remember receiving contact from a fat Asian man with a very pompous on-line name standing beside a red Porsche with blacked out number plates. Finding him utterly revolting I deleted him immediately thinking he should have advertised his wares on a sugar daddy site. I have been saddened by the men who are photographed with their laundry in the background - like how unromantic is that? God, guys get a grip on yourselves. If you want a good woman, put your best foot forward. And men, just before I leave this topic, don't post the photo at your daughter's wedding in the hired Tux or the one with your ex's arm just visible before you cut her out. Spend some dollars investing in a great photo to show us who you are and iron your clothes before it's taken: we deserve it!

Ladies, be aware of how you judge others and make sure you are impeccable in that way. Clients are always telling me that spelling and grammar make a huge difference in their choice of men on the net. It does for me too. When a schoolteacher I was corresponding with said he was a "domestic sole" I wondered if he would serve himself up with lemon wedges and chips! If he was he wanting a sole mate it certainly wasn't me! And guys for heaven's sake get the difference between "your" and "you're" - they will never be the same for most of us and yes, we do judge you on your potential to be our mate if you can't spell! Poor punctuation, lack of capitalisations and other grammatical errors also tell a story and are off-putting for lots of us.

We'll talk about lies and deceptions later and highlight what I call Red Flags who are men you need to steer clear of, but for now let's focus on what else you put in your on-line profile.

Marking down what your habits are and what you are looking for is a huge giveaway. A man or woman who has nothing in the "ideal mate specification", and I've seen lots of them, will never know when they have hit the bull's eye because they don't know what they want. So put something in and be general unless you absolutely know what you want. Make it the truth or else you will be caught out.

But don't let it be so much of the truth that it is utterly boring. Like the man who contacted me with the heading "worth it, or maybe not????" and then proceeded to say he was insecure, had no goals or direction, was a couch potato, not good looking with a poor sense of humour, and didn't know the reason for his *exsistence* (sic). Now even if he was joking on all that he goes on to say he's too considerate of other's needs and too much of a pleaser. What he had in his ideal mate profile was Not Important for just about everything other than age when he said he wanted a woman from 40 - 60. He was just 43. How could any good woman seriously be interested in wasting a moment's time on someone like this? Red Flag? Yes, you bet!

Alicia and Roger were living together and talking marriage when her friend alerted her to the appearance of his profile on a dating site. Without ado she threw him out that day and opened a bottle of Bollinger to celebrate. Later she had a huge laugh over the inconsistencies in his on-line profile. He declared that live theatre was one of his interests but she knew he hadn't been near an entertainment centre since he played in third rate rock bands 25 years before. That he "absolutely hated television" gave her a giggle knowing that the first thing he did every morning was turn on the TV and his statement that he loved travel had her in fits of laughter knowing he'd never ever left the country. Presumably some poor soul would have believed all these lies and contacted him on the basis of them. For those in the know, Roger is definitely a Red Flag.

44

I've met some men who state they are occasional smokers when they smoke a packet a day and "occasional drinkers" when they drink a bottle of wine a day and I wonder whether they believe it or are just trying to fool others. Max's identity as a serious binge drinker came to light only after he spent the night in a lock-up and subsequently lost his driving licence. Prior to that, his new date, Jenny, believed he was only a social drinker. Red Flag? Yes, I think so!

The important thing here is to write a light and truthful profile and then to know how to assess the profiles of men who contact you.

Think about how you vet men on the internet. What is the thing that attracts you first? It is his looks, his profile, his education, the type of job he has, his marital status, that he either has or doesn't have kids? What is it?

You need to know that. I was first introduced to internet dating after I left my husband a few years ago through a girlfriend I was walking with one day. She was going to a wedding that weekend of a couple who had met on the net. The bride had vetted all the men on their educational level; for her they had to have at least an undergraduate degree, and he had one. Good luck to her, she knew what she wanted and she found it.

There are so many men out there that I think you should know what you want, otherwise you will be inundated with offers and it will be overwhelming. 28-year-old Lucy, a gorgeous brunette, is not really clear what she wants and when she went on line she had dozens of responses overnight. Totally overwhelmed, she hid her profile and went out with some girlfriends instead. She tells me that her 20's girlfriends get 80 - 100 hits in a day.

> **It is funny about life: it you refuse to accept anything but the very best you will very often get it.   W. Somerset Maugham**

My single clients want a man who has not had children since they want to have kids. My divorced friends would not entertain the thought of a man who had not had children because he would not know what it is like to be a parent and the place she needs to make in her life for her kids and maybe grandkids.

You also need to know what puts you off when a man contacts you. Sometimes, be honest, it's his photograph. Sometimes it's his pseudonym - too boring, too egotistical, too sexy. Sometimes it is his educational level, or his spelling, or his absolute lack of clarity about what he wants. Whatever it is, use that as a Red Flag and opt out then. Save yourself the grief - not hard to do when you know in advance what you don't want! Make this choice be a real choice; go for a relationship by design not default. There will be enough of what you don't want in any relationship - after all, we are there to be each other's greatest teachers, so there will always stuff we don't want. Don't add to it by settling up front with things you know you can't live with.

> **It is our choices that show what we truly are, far more than our abilities.   J.K. Rowling**

And to be fair, you won't get clarity on some things until you have gone out with him. I remember a first date with David, all going swimmingly until he told me he'd left hospital the day before after major heart surgery! Please!!! Or John, the lawyer, who wanted to play golf four days a week when I'm still cranking up my career. Or Vince the Garden Gnome who went out with a friend who asked him what he planned to be doing in 30 years and he said "I'll be dead!"

And as a final word there are many things not obvious on dating sites that are important such as what sort of relationship do they have with their ex spouse, if they have decent relationships with their kids, what their job history is like, when their last long term relationship ended and what sort of financial capacity do they have to enter into a committed and exclusive relationship. That last one is a biggie, because men are always telling me how poorly they come out of divorces with often 70% of their net worth going to their spouse and no matter what they would like to do, they simply do not have the financial resources to create another long term and permanent relationship. These things we need to know and assess before we give our hearts away, don't we ladies?

47

NOTE TO SELF:

♥   I'll choose a great name and picture that shows who I am

♥   I'll write an honest profile including what I'll bring to the relationship

♥   I'll learn to read men's profiles and decide what I want and what I don't want

CHAPTER SEVEN

NAVIGATING THROUGH THE PRE-DATING MAZE

Once the interest starts filtering into your in-box you have to decide how you intend to proceed in the dating game. If you are half good looking you will have dozens of contacts on day one and it could be overwhelming. If it's been a while since you were in a relationship or had a date, you are likely to be very confused or, in some cases, fearful.

Fifteen years ago a man received an average of 750 rejections in his dating life and without a doubt that has significantly increased since internet dating. And now women too are faced with rejection in a different way from previous dating games. To send a message to someone over the net takes most people out of their comfort zone. To be rejected by someone you don't even know is horrible; to be ignored is a big blow to the ego and the morale.

Fundamentally, overwhelm, confusion and fear of rejection are all likely to put you in a tail spin unless you have some defined protocols that will put the whole process in some sort of order. Notice that I don't say "rules" here because I have a very definite belief that, in a relationship, rules will always only make another person wrong, and this book is designed to give you a much better way to create and maintain a lasting love relationship, not fracture it from day one. Let's go through some protocols that will give you a guide to internet dating on your terms.

I believe that if you want a man who is in his masculine energy - ie the hunter, then you should not be the first to approach him either in chat rooms or on internet dating sites. Let him do the work and show you who he really is.

Some men are notoriously lazy and have seriously been spoilt by ladies who do everything for them. This is not recommended if you don't want to bemoan their lack of action for the rest of the relationship life. You may be thinking that this means you are taking the back seat, and guess what, you are. You don't have to do anything! Leaving the contacting and the organising up to him will let you know quickly if he is in his masculine energy or not and how safe it will be for you to reside in your feminine energy. This is a big change from how most modern women do the rest of their lives: doing this, doing that, juggling work and mortgage payments, trying to fix the plumbing and the car, always doing stuff. Ladies, you are not human doings.....you are human beings so relax, have fun and lighten up. This is what he wants and when you get used to it, you will love it too, unless you want to control him.

I'll say it again, what he will fall in love with is your radiance. If you are perpetually in do-do-do mode, your radiance will have left town. Believe me, this is the truth. So do nothing. Approach no one. And know that whoever is truly interested in you will find you. I hope I hear you saying "oh what a relief!" and yes it will be. Trust me that men still want to be hunters...the good ones that is, and that's the least you want and should expect. Right? The 1st

Protocol then is to let him approach you with whatever the modality is that your dating site provides for a first contact.

When and how to respond is Protocol 2. No matter how good he looks or how connected you feel to what he has written, do nothing for 24 hours. Remember men like to hunt and if they catch their first prey too easily they do not enjoy that victory. So if you receive the first contact during work hours, respond a day later. However, once you leave your office on a Friday night you will not even go on line to look at your dating site until Monday afternoon and you will certainly not respond to a new admirer. Why you ask? Surely it's too obvious to state? There are millions of people on the net trying to find a partner. If you are available on a Friday or Saturday night when most people are either out on a date or having fun doing something else they love, he will see you as less-than; a bit of a reject....not desired by someone else. He may not know the truth, that you are hot as hell or that you've just joined up on the site, or moved to town or whatever. All he'll know is that you are alone with your laptop when everyone else is painting the town red.

If he sees you as desperate he is instantly turned off. Men love to be needed but they don't want you to be needy. So you need to be really aware of creating some protocols for yourself around when you are on line and we'll talk more about that in Protocol 3.

Men like and need a challenge. It's what they all do during their day jobs. There is always a report to write, a challenging meeting to attend, a marketing strategy to create, someone to hire or fire or a difficult client to placate. That's what men are hard wired to do well. It's in their DNA. So don't take their job away from them or you will regret it for ever.

So after a gap of 24 hours, or the weekend if he approaches you later than Friday afternoon, respond with a yes if you like the look of him. If you respond by email, make it very brief like "thanks for your contact, I look forward to receiving an email from you". Don't tell him anything else, like you think he looks cute or you have the same hobbies or that he reminds you of your brother or you have a similar profession. All too much information and not giving him the space to dig the details out of you! And of course if he doesn't appeal to you, do nothing. Delete him and move on or be polite and say no thanks.

Protocol No 3 is about when you're on line. If you want to show a man you don't have a life and that you are desperate for him to whisk you away, you will be on line at any time of the day or night, weekdays, weekends and holidays. If you want to be a bit exclusive, you will have some strong boundaries around when you are on line. This will not include late at night, in the middle of the night (if you can't sleep listen to some beautiful music instead), anytime from Friday afternoon to Monday afternoon, holidays or too early in the morning. Most dating sites show when you've last been on line; spacing it out a bit means you don't appear too eager.

If you don't have boundaries, you will fill your relationship with rules that make the other person wrong.

Men like you to be a bit hard to get. Well, part of them wants you to be easy, but they tell me time and time again that a no-challenge girl who comes over with the lot too easily is actually a huge disappointment to them. Believe them!

The interesting thing is that men are often on line late at night (maybe after a disappointing date) but certainly because that's the time they want sex. If you go on line to chat with them then not only are you likely to be asked some questions that, for you, will ruin the prospects of a relationship, but if you do go ahead with it, their thoughts of you will be linked and anchored to their desire for sex and the real relationship you want may never get off the ground. When men initiate contact between midnight and 7am I suggest you leave them alone for it would appear they don't have much of a life. Sunday morning is another time men get on the internet to check out women which is another reason to leave your laptop alone during weekends when you should be out doing something more interesting! Let them know you've got a life and if you truly have something to offer a relationship, you will have a life. You'll have family and friends, a career, something else you are passionate about, maybe sport or exercise or shopping. Whatever it is, have a balanced life before you go shopping for a man otherwise he will see you as a Red Flag.

Protocol 4 is how you decide whether you want to meet him or not. You must know your boundaries around this. You have after all spent some time creating a profile that says what you want, so don't ignore it when you get interest from men. You are still in the information gathering phase and if you are feeling something that really puts you off consider it a Red Flag. He may have said something that you consciously don't want or you may just get a sort of gut reaction. Ladies, we used to be burnt at the stake for our gut reactions (when men thought we were witches) so take note of them. They are probably absolutely valid and you would be wise to act upon them every single time.

You are, after all, looking for a man to spend the rest of your life with, perhaps be the father of your children. So in these early stages before you are remotely attached you must get very clear about what is acceptable and what is not. Is his voice something you could listen to for ever? If it's not, then don't date him. Has he made casual and inappropriate references to sex during your three or four emails? If he has, don't date him. Has he given you a blow by blow description of why his last relationship didn't work? If he did, don't date him. If he's asked you inappropriate questions like how much you earn or how come you're still single, don't date him. If he's declared his undying love before you meet, don't meet, he's in fantasyland and is probably narcissistic.

Has his behaviour been hot and cold ... eager to see you one minute and then ignoring you the next? And if he has and you don't like it, don't date him .... it will get worse. Some men do this. They get carried away with an initial communication and

54

then you don't hear from them for a few weeks. Sometimes this happens after you have shared considerable communication and felt a real connection with him. Sometimes he has even told you he will call you and he does not. Sometimes he hides his profile, going off line. If he comes back, ignore him. Do not say yes to this guy. He's already made you feel yucky; don't beat yourself up by going back for another burst. It is likely he is a card carrying self-saboteur which is a great reason to avoid him and you'll read more about his habits in Mr Remote.

There are lots of other reasons to say no. Basically if you don't feel good about it, err on the side of caution by saying no. We all have a bunch of reasons that are personal and all I ask is that you trust your inner guidance about these things. If you have a strong "No" coming up, then say no and move on. Life should be about fun and joy, not asking for grief from someone whom you don't even know.

> **If you are going through hell, keep going. Churchill**

Whilst we are on the subject of your gut, let's move to Protocol 5 which is about choosing men who zap you rather than sap you. I have a strong belief that energy connects us in the first place, and that energy will determine whether it's a good one or a bad one. You want to be zapped by your man; you want to be made to feel more alive, not less alive. Keep your energy field clean by going out with men who make you feel alive, not those who sap you. So be selective. You know what you want; and if you don't know then it's the opposite of what you don't want, so don't waste time with guys who aren't what you want in the big things that really matter to you.

If you want kids and he says he doesn't, think about that. If he's never been married, he'll probably be happy to have kids with the right women who has so far not shown up in his life. If he's been married, has kids and says no to more, it's probably financial.

If you want a man with a tertiary qualification, it's no doubt because you have a brain and enjoy intelligence conversation. Maybe intelligence is one of your top values. So you may want to pass on the tradies or people who haven't finished high school unless their profile indicates a hidden brilliance that was obtained at the University of Life rather than in the school grounds. If you are a practising catholic then probably an atheist would not work as a long term partner. If you are an active business person then someone who is into retirement and playing golf 4 days a week would probably bore you to tears.

Think about it. It is different for every one of you. You don't have to compromise wildly on things that are really important to you. Look at how his profile matches yours and choose to move on from those where there is a mismatch of something really major and important to you. For the smaller things, let it go. After all, similarities create a great relationship and differences create real passion, so it's a toss-up anyway. Just don't try and join the dots before you've met him and pretend that this thing you don't like is not important. If it's on your profile it IS important to you. So use your intuition and if it's not right don't let him sap you. Find a man to zap you!

The trouble is, he has probably not read your profile properly anyway, which means he is not selecting you on every piece of matching interest or information. So if what he says on his profile or what you get from the initial emails or phone conversations doesn't match your deepest desires, move on. The universe always has a back-up plan! There is more than one guy for you!

Protocol 6 is moving to the date and giving him your personal details. Presuming you responded with a yes, he should then get back to you pretty quickly with an invitation to meet. How long this takes and how it happens can either be a green flag to go along or a red flag to delete this man and move on.

He should be asking you some questions about you and if you are interested in him your answers should be brief and not too revealing. Remember you are getting him to work at this.....and whatever happens in the beginning is how the relationship will go for life. So it's very important you get it right.

If you give him everything on a platter, you will be just like most of the other girls out there and will be immediately forgettable. If you want him to continue with this initial communication keep a bit of mystery in your answers .... whatever you do don't reveal all or he will be bored by the chase and move on.

Within two or three emails there should be progress towards a date

Within two or three emails there should be progress towards a date. If there is not, then do nothing and see what happens. Certainly it is his job to ask you out, just as if you were at a party or in a wine bar. This is not the time you start to plan your next weekend and include him. It's a clear case of His Job!

Remember she who flirts first is female: he who speaks first is male. Decide which you want to be, and flirt a little whilst waiting for him to ask you out. If he doesn't ask you out within the first couple of weeks, if you live in the same town, then I'd want you to Red Flag him.

How he arranges the first date is important. If he arranges it by text he will be likely to end the relationship by text. Watch out for this and read more in the chapter on Mr Cyber Freak.

He may ask for your phone number so you can talk before he asks you for a date. Many men don't these days; they think that the internet is just as good as a phone so don't be overly concerned if your first date is arranged by email. Unless you need to hear his voice first, in which case you need to ask him to call you if he doesn't volunteer to do so.

Often he'll give you his phone number first. Many men think that a girl will not want to disclose her number to someone she has met on an internet dating site. However, if you think he's ok and he wants to arrange a date then by all means give him your mobile number, not your office or your home number. At least then you will be able to hear his voice and decide if it's something you could live with forever. If it's not, then decline the date and wish him well in his search. He'll get over it and so will you. Move on!

Don't give him other personal details such as your home address, your work details or other personal particulars. Whilst we like to assume everyone is decent, there are weirdos out there and you need to be safe. It's pretty obvious what's sensible and what's not, so be sensible and you'll be safe.

The phone call also has another dimension. Going back to our forebears it was the man who did stuff for the woman. He was the hunter and she was provided for. Whilst life has changed dramatically I have yet to meet a woman who doesn't want her mate to be a hunter. I also know that what he will do to get his first date is his pattern for the entire relationship unless something shocks him into a new reality.

Preferring to stay in feminine energy you'll do best to respond rather than initiate so not only will you let him call you, you will let him be the one to suggest the first date. If, like Mario, the photographer who said he'd ring Liz twice, once when they connected on the internet and another after they came face to face at a legal function, they fail to ring, they are relegated to Red Flag status. If they ring within five minutes of having your phone number, you will be impressed and they will have half a chance. Dave did this when Jen gave him her number. They had a pleasant conversation, discovered some things they both liked doing such as sailing but then he broke off suddenly saying can I call you tomorrow, I have a meeting? Jen was surprised when an email popped into her box minutes later saying she was not the one for him. Thinking back on the conversation, which was mostly about him, she felt a happy release from a boring and dominating man!

Girls, as an aside, if you meet him at a bar, a club, a conference or in the lift and he gives you his business card saying "give me a ring", please reply with "I don't think so" and give it smartly back to him with the best smile you can manage. A man in his masculine drive can always get your details and step up to the plate. Because that is what you want him to do for you, isn't it?

The length of time you communicate before he arranges the first date is Protocol 7. The thing about internet dating is that there is a complete smorgasbord out there: men and women around the country and around the world, thousands of them that look great and could be your ideal mate. When you read on about the men to avoid and why, more details will emerge that will Red Flag a

60

problem, but for now know that this is a big one. Men like variety. They are highly visual creatures, they are turned on by looks, and they will be in contact with a considerable number of women at once. He'll barely differentiate between them and he'll want to keep them all on the go until he has a reason to choose. If indeed he does choose. Many don't. They contact many women, many women contact them and they do nothing. If he has not asked you out and arranged a date by email 3 or 4 then move on. Sitting in your office or your home emailing someone you'd like to meet and perhaps have a relationship with is no substitute for the real thing. Some will choose to meet you, and because they have so many women on the go at the same time their limited resources dictate that all the meetings are coffee only. That's OK but if it's only coffee the second time that must be your next Red Flag. Move on and make room to be with someone who is keen to buy you lunch or dinner and get to know you over several hours not just the time it takes to consume a latte.

Protocol 8 is about availability. When deciding to date you must be emotionally available. That's a given. Yes, we all have baggage, but know in your heart that you are ready to give and to love without bounds: that you are not still clinging on to the last man in your life or the one before. Know that you are emotionally free, and ready to love again even if it means you get hurt. But be not available too quickly in the practical sense. What I mean is if he asks you out on a Friday for a Saturday night, you must know that you are probably his third choice. It's better to stay home yet another Saturday night if you must than be so eager that you say yes to a last minute invitation. Make it so that he has to work for you. Tuesday or at the latest Wednesday is fine, anything after that is too late and must be refused, even if you are dying to meet him: especially if you are dying to meet him! Curb your passion, your anxiety and make him work for you. If he's really keen to meet he will ask you out with more notice the next time. If he doesn't he's another Red Flag.

You'll need Protocol 9 to go on your first date. If you like the sound of the voice and he's been polite, interested and consistent in his communications, then by all means arrange to meet. Once you have made the date, don't ring, email or text him unless you need to change it. Then for meeting you know the rules: in a well lit place, busy street, recognised bar or coffee shop etc. Not at his place, not at yours, not anywhere that's dark and spooky. All this makes sense and it's not difficult to work out what feels right and what does not. Take your own car; don't park directly in front of where you are meeting and tell someone where you are going and with whom. As to what the first date should consist of, that's in the next chapter.

Continuing communication after the first date is the subject of Protocol 10. It's incredibly simple: don't email him or ring him. You will have thanked him for the date when you parted so you don't need to text him to say thank you again. You need to leave the ball back with him to take the next step. This is because you need to know if he is interested and if you are the one that keeps the communication going, how will you ever know if he really likes you and wants a relationship with you? How will you know if you are simply a diversion and an easy social and or sexual partner? How will you know how he feels about you if you take over his job? I know how he will feel about you, he will feel cheated, he will feel flat and he will have the wind taken out of his sails because if he's decided to pursue you, he wants to do it on his own terms. And if he's not interested and doesn't call, you have saved yourself the embarrassment of calling him and finding him uninterested in asking you out again. So you must do nothing. No phone calls. No texts. No emails. Until you hear from him and he wants to see you again.

Hopefully he'll call you rather than text you to ask for the next date. In some ways today's communications blur the edges of relationships. Before mobile phones and text messages, he would bring you flowers (I said bring, not send) if he was really out to make an impression. Now you think you're lucky if you get a text. Personally I like to hear a voice, it's much more sincere. About 38% of our communication is perceived through voice qualities and if you're attuned to picking up the subtleties of his communication you won't be happy with the anonymity of a text message.

If he calls and you miss him, don't instantly return his call, and when you do – later – don't apologise for not doing it instantly. Remain a bit indifferent if you really like him. This requires effort, patience and self restraint. You don't have to be impossible to get – just hard to get, and if phoning you is not always successful then he might get to ask you out each time your previous date ends – then you really know he's interested.

And as an afterthought, always be the one to end the conversation on the phone – if you leave him dangling a bit he'll most likely be keener. Don't appear you have nothing to do but talk to him and again don't /not ever /never give explanations. Just do a "must fly, see you Saturday" sort of parting.

And if you don't hear from him, continue to do nothing

And if you don't hear from him, continue to do nothing. Don't call with some feeble excuse about how your phone has been out of action, or your internet not working. If he's interested, he will move mountains to keep in touch. And it may not be the day after the date. So keep busy, get with some girlfriends, have a massage, go for a long walk on the beach; anything but pick up that phone of yours! Got it? And congratulate yourself for your strength and your standards.

NOTE TO SELF

♥   **I'll practice the protocols that allow him to be in his masculine energy**

♥   **I'll stay off line during evenings and weekends**

♥   **I will only meet up when I feel comfortable doing so**

CHAPTER EIGHT

DATING ON YOUR TERMS

He's finally got to ask you out. Now you can begin to find out what he is really like, starting with how and where he suggests you meet. Arranging a date is his job. And since this is the real beginning of your exploratory expedition, it will tell you heaps about him. It will also tell you how savvy he is as a man. Like does he really know where to take you, is it a nice place you'd go to with friends, it is public or has he suggested his pad or calling in at your home.

The first date is an opportunity for you to evaluate the man so you need to start where you intend to proceed. Given you have gone through a rigorous selection process to get this far, don't necessarily settle for a cup of coffee. If he only asks you for a coffee, then you could presume (a) he has many other women on the go or (b) he does not want to spend money on finding out who you are or (c) he is only marginally interested in you. Coffee is to catch up with your girlfriends or report in on your latest date, not to have the latest date because it won't give you as much insight into him as sharing a meal with him will but if that's all he suggests, then go for it if you're interested in meeting him.

Whatever you do, don't agree to a first date which feels in some way inappropriate; drinks late at night, anything at his house, somewhere too close to your home, inviting himself to your home or in a pub amongst a group of his friends. These are all Red Flags and if he's reluctant to offer a better choice then give him a miss and move on.

Some clients tell me they don't do the coffee thing. They want to have lunch or dinner on the first date to see how things go over a meal: how he eats, what he eats and whether he holds his knife and fork the way they like. Other clients say the coffee thing works well because if he's awful they can leave soon. I think if you have done your homework properly you won't want to leave soon and in any event, I feel a slightly longer meeting is perfect for the first date. In 2-3 hours you can assess someone pretty well. You can look at how easily the conversation flows, or not, how much he talks about himself or whether he asks about you, how much eye contact he gives you and whether you feel there is anything going for you. You will be able to quickly ascertain how far from his profile he is: it will range from spot on to nothing like what you have read about him, and that should give you some warning bells too. And if he is not the one for you, then the 2-3 hours you have spent with him will have taught you some very valuable things about yourself to take into the next meeting. You will also know how he treats a lady by looking after her drinks, pouring the water, and making sure he puts his attention onto her needs. And of course how he treats the waiters is how he'll treat you some time so watch out for that!

Then there is the interesting question of who pays. Now in my book, that's also his job. He has had the pleasure of your company, he invited you out in the first place and he pays.

Always. So when the bill comes, you just sit tight and smile and thank him for a lovely time. That's easy even when you are not used to doing it. And for the record ladies, there is nothing you have to do in return. Remember the formula to captivate this man is to be feminine, enchanting and authentic. For him to appeal to you he must take the lead – that's what a real man does. If he asks you on a date, he is expected to pay for the pleasure of your company and that is all that you have to give to him. Men have to understand that if they want a woman, they have to pay for her. Going Dutch is reserved for friends and work mates, not a man who has invited you out; this is not a time to make a stance on being equal. It is not a case of equality it's a case of etiquette. Women at my workshops have often said they feel if he pays they have to provide sex in return. That is SO not the truth. You have given him the pleasure of your company and that is all that is required at this stage. Not a thing more or you are taking over his job. Remember he is the hunter and you the hunted. So if he expects you to pay, you simply tell him that since he invited you out, you believed he would be paying for you, and smile your sweetest smile. He will get it and both of you will get that he has been spoiled by too many women. You will set yourself apart as a woman who deserves to be treated well and has standards. And remember, how you start this relationship is how it will proceed. It's very difficult to go back and set new ground rules once you are in mid-stream.

.

And if it is coffee, and then he suggests you move on for dinner or drinks, say no. You have agreed (to yourself) that you will give him an absolute maximum of 2 hours, so stick to that. If you extend it he will think you haven't a better offer and you become less attractive and more of a chance for sex that night. If he wants to see you again he will ask, so excuse yourself without saying why and let him step up to the plate and ask you out again. My client Sandy warns against alcohol on the first date from an experience she regrets. Meeting Christian for the first time, she found him attractive and engaging so when he plied her with liquor she was an easy bed mate for him that night. In the morning she realised how stupid she had been: she felt ill, she hated herself for having sex with someone she barely knew, she couldn't wait to get home, and of course she never heard from him again.

> **Loving is like playing the violin: first learn the rules, then forget and play from your heart.   Dr Buzz McCarthy**

Whether he's going be the The One for you or not, you can hone your dating skills with him so decide to enjoy the date you're on. It's an opportunity to find out about him and what he values most and you should be initiating questions that elicit this information. Don't reveal your life history, the gory details of your former relationships and how badly your ex treated you. You will find out each other's flaws soon enough so leave the years of therapy alone on the first dates, you don't need to know how each other has messed up before! This is the time to have fun and let your light shine not a time to be serious and boring. And you don't have to astound him with your achievements unless you're looking for a business partner! Dating is not therapy and whatever else you do, don't try and 'fix him': it's arrogant, impossible, won't work and will dampen his spirit. Be alert for a date who only talks about

68

himself; if he is not interested in who you are and what makes you tick he's a Red Flag and it is time to move on to the next opportunity.

The most valuable conversation you can have with a man on your first date is to find out what he values most as this will give you a big clue as to whether you have a future together or not. Ask him some of these questions and store the answers in your head.

1. How do you spend your time? (Clue: how he spends his money and if he is financially abundant or challenged)

2. Is your job something you are passionate about? (Clue: does he go for what he wants or is he prepared to settle?)

3. What do you think about most? (Clue: is he practical or a dreamer?)

4. What do you talk to others about most? (Clue: how open he is.)

5. Who is your best friend and what do you love about them? (Clue: are his friends important and does he easily have access to feelings.)

6. How easy is it for you to write your goals? (Clue: does he have any and how committed is he to them?)

7. If money, time and health were no barrier how would you spend the rest of your life? (Clue: what does he want his life to be like?)

So the evening is over and he was (a) boring, (b) self focussed (c) not really interested in finding out about you (d) brought up inappropriate conversation such as his sex life (e) asked you about yours (f) touched you inappropriately or (g) you got a funny feeling that he was a phony, then you can Red Flag him, thank him for the evening and move on. If he invites you out again, simply say "no thanks I don't think we have enough in common". It's not difficult to do and good practice to learn to speak your truth. Don't agree to a second date if he didn't rock your boat and if think you're not sure, you are sure he is not the one. Trust your intuition.

Or if it's a good scenario and you've had a pleasant time with him so what happens next? You thank him and when he asks to see you again say yes and that you look forward to him calling you to arrange something. That's it; then off you go. No kissing and certainly no sex!

If the second date is a suggestion to hang out with his mates, yet another coffee date, dinner at his place or yours, if he asks you to join him at another function where you are not the main event or he asks you to go away for a weekend, decline and depending on how readily or not he suggests something more appropriate you may want to Red Flag him. His place means you are a sexual target, so does yours. If he wants to hang out with his mates or go to a function, you are not going to focus on getting to know each other it is going to be more social. If it was coffee first up, then you progress to a meal. If it was a meal, it is another meal, out at a restaurant. Don't feel you have to immediately reciprocate and

70

certainly don't invite him back to your place for dinner. He will think you are taking control or mothering him and he will also think it's an invitation to bed and that should not yet be on your agenda!

Remember you still don't know him and you must still be in the public arena. People hide their flaws for a very long time so keep your head on and be safe and sensible. Don't think that because he's a lawyer, he will be honourable. In my university days I attended a debate at Long Bay Jail in Sydney and one of the teams was made up entirely of lawyers.... all in jail uniform and drinking tea out of tin mugs. Keep your head on...and your knickers, but more on that later!

So you decide you like him enough to have a second date and you are still receiving contacts from others on the internet. What do you do?

Let me tell you my theory on options: I believe that there is only an option when there are three choices. Having one choice is no choice, right? If you have two choices, you will go for the least worst because there may be no clear winner. Only when you have three choices is there a real option or a good, better and best. So I recommend that you date three men at the same time until you decide that one stands out and you would like to pursue that relationship. Three are enough to manage in your busy life without getting confused or falling in the trap that my client Charlotte did.

A divorcee in her 40's Charlotte, a business consultant, was dating five men at the same time. Two of them she didn't see as long term prospects but enjoyed their company. One she adored but he was married. Another was an old flame back on the scene and the fifth was a potential business partner with whom she had crossed the line. With all these men, Charlotte was taking the lead. She was ringing them, inviting them to dinner, organising movies, and in between the coffees texting them to connect on a regular basis. When I allowed her to see that she had taken on the masculine role she was completely shocked. In encouraging her to access more of her feminine and be less in control I suggested that she stop initiating any communication and let the men take the lead. They did. Well a couple of them. Two fell by the wayside, the business potential turned out to be a wimp, the old flame died out, and the married man she cared for went back to his wife. The other dynamic of significance to Charlotte was that in dating five men each put into the mix one thing she needed. As they fell away like a pack of cards, she realised that none had anywhere near everything she wanted. So with the clarity of knowing those five qualities, she knew exactly what she wanted in just one man.

So even if you like him you should stay on line, communicate with other men and select another two to date. Know that he will too. Have fun getting to know another couple of men, let them do all the organising, all the contacting, and remember not to answer their messages too soon, remember not to initiate messages and remember to consciously tick the boxes on your Must Have list. You are still in information gathering mode and you are still testing him to see how he shows up for you and until you really decide for yourself who has a greater likelihood of being what you want, let them all take the initiative. And when you come across Red Flags, you know to move on.

Let's say you've been out with someone a few times and then you don't hear from him again, my advice is to do nothing. If you chase him, you will never really be sure if you are Miss Right for him or an easy Miss Right Now. If you don't care, ring all you like and risk even more disappointment. If you have standards, do nothing.

If, after a couple of dates when you have gathered lots of information on him but you still can't tick the top ten Must Have's on your list, it's time to move on to the next one. Don't fall back on the fear that there is no-one else out there and this one will do. Don't pretend those Must Have's are not important for you; if you know in your heart that it is not right, choose to move on with the full knowledge that the universe provides a back-up plan.... there is always someone else out there for you provided you stay in the game.

> **I have not failed. I've just found 10,000 ways that won't work.**
> **Thomas Alva Edison**

For now, its date three guys at once, keep your profile on line, keep in the public arena, don't feel you have to reciprocate in any way and stay out of any bedroom. This is absolutely a time for no sex. Even if you want it and haven't had it for ages, you can wait a bit longer. So can he! Just keep it light, breezy and collect as much information both consciously and unconsciously about him to make a real assessment as to whether this relationship has the potential to be exclusive, committed, loving and passionate for the rest of your life.

NOTE TO SELF:

♥ **I don't have to say yes to them all: I know the universe has a back-up plan**

♥ **I will work out what sort of date works for me and I'll stick to it**

♥ **I commit to asking lots of questions that will show me who he really is**

CHAPTER NINE

MEN TO AVOID

All the women I know and work with want healthy, loving, committed relationships. Many of them have done some work on themselves and most have had enough disastrous relationships to know what they want and what they are no longer prepared to settle for.

Some have been married, many not. Some have lived with guys and it hasn't worked. Some have kids and many want to have kids. They are all decent women who treat people well and want to be loved, honoured and cherished by their partner. These are not women who want instant sex or multiple partners. They want a relationship where they and their partner share some important values, can plan a great life and experience many magic moments together for a long time.

None of what they want is out of the ordinary. Whether they are in their 20's or their 60's these women want a partner now, not next year or next decade. They want to get on with their lives and they understand that the internet provides them with a greater choice of prospective partners than almost anywhere else.

But what they don't want is to be screwed around by a guy or a bunch of guys they don't even know. So the following 9 chapters are written to help them identify and steer clear of some kinds of men. It's not that these men are bad men (well most of them are not) but some of their behaviour doesn't make these ladies feel good about being in relationship with them. Some string them along because they can't really afford a woman, some are emotionally unavailable, some are desperate to find a perfect woman, many only want sex, some hide behind the anonymity of cyberspace, some have no clue what they want and are total time wasters, some have addictions that make a relationship not viable, some are married and cheating, some are liars and some are predators.

If it hurts it isn't love.   Chuck Spezzano

For a good woman wanting an outstanding relationship no men in these categories are worth spending any time on. These chapters will help you recognise them quickly so you can Red Flag them and move on to someone more suitable.

I have identified these men as:

1.   **Mr Unavailable**
     "I'm so ready for love again"

2.   **Mr Desperate Dan**
     "You mean you don't care if I am 20 or 45?"

3.   **Mr Sex Only**
     "Can you send me a pic?"

4.   **Mr Cheater**
     "My wife/girlfriend and I don't have sex anymore"

5.   **Mr Addict**
     "I'm not sure you are everything I want"

6.   **Mr Remote**
     "Now you see me, now you don't"

7.   **Mr Cyber Freak**
     "What do you mean, do I have msn?

8.   **Mr Blatant Liar**
     "I didn't realise my profile was still visible"

9.   **Mr Predator**
     "Where do you want me to send that money?"

Then there is Mr Right - your Prince of Princes and when you think it's hopeless, you'll find him in the following chapter.

NOTE TO SELF:

♥   **I'll use the Mr Men profiles to evaluate who contacts me**

♥   **Then I'll use my intuition to add to the picture before I continue**

♥   **I understand that saying no clears the energy for Mr Right to show up**

CHAPTER TEN

MR UNAVAILABLE

A sure fire way to relationship disaster is to get involved with a man who is simply not available for a woman who wants a real relationship. There are a number of different types of men in this category and all of them are Red Flags for those wanting a lasting and committed relationship.

The first type has very recently left a long term relationship and I will call him Mr Just Out. No matter what he might say to you, he is not ready for the commitment you want. I must emphasise that when he says "I'm ready" to you, you must be on high alert. When he says he's ready, he means a whole lot of other things. These will range from "I'm ready for some sex again", or "I want to take you to dinner" which means he's sick of trying to cook for himself, or "I'd love you to cook for me at your house" which means he wants the sex and the dinner, and probably in that order.

The generally accepted fact is that men are pretty hopeless on their own after being in a long term relationship. In short, they are lost. Not just in the practical things of life, they really lose their masculine purpose and their lives quite often really fall apart. They lose all their power, they don't look after themselves, they drink too much, they don't eat properly and they don't talk to anyone about what happened. They bottle it up and hope it goes away. Then they try to offload some of the grief onto the next woman who crosses their path. If she's sensible she will steer clear; if she's not then she will easily fall into the role of rescuer to his victim and neither of them will prosper. It's Red Flag territory for women who want a real relationship.

The tolerance level for men out of a long term relationship, before they start looking for someone else is about 5 weeks. Interestingly research shows that men need 3 years to get over a long relationship but most are re-partnered within one year. And since most marriages are ended by the wife these days I believe many of the ex husbands settle for someone who is less than what they want after being chucked out of a marriage whereas most women I talk to want something much better, not equal to and certainly not worse.

But men are not as choosy and have that need to prove themselves again, very quickly, so fragile are their egos. And if you are there, you can easily be hoodwinked into thinking that this is the man for you. Trust me, he won't be.

I have found that men just out of a relationship often tend to lie about how long they have been on their own. My client Sally, a travel agent in her 30's, told me when she met her future husband Steve told her he'd been separated from his former wife for 6 months. Only 3 years later when she saw their marriage licence the week before their nuptials did she realise he had been on his own for only 6 weeks when they met. She said that had known the truth she would not have entered into an intimate relationship with him so soon after a 12+ year marriage. Interestingly 5 weeks after she left him he was ringing women advertising in the lonely hearts club section of the daily newspaper which she felt was very demeaning after their 21 years together. And I bet he didn't tell any of them the truth either.

It is suggested by some experts that you should be on your own for one month for every year of your committed relationship. So, in Sally's case, she and Steve both should have been partnerless for 21 months. It doesn't happen for many men who partner usually within a year although they often won't marry the new woman and yes, it happened in Steve's case. He got into a relationship after a few months of being on his own, moved interstate to the new woman but wouldn't marry her.

The problem with pairing up so soon is that you don't have time to process the end of the relationship. No matter who ended it, if it was significant either in terms of time or commitment, or both, both partners need time to unpick it from an emotional perspective so they can move on with more clarity and less baggage.

There will always be disappointment or sadness that your vision of a life together did not happen. If there is an affair which ends the marriage, then there will probably be guilt for one and anger for the other partner. If there is abuse or addictions, there will probably be anger from both sides to add to the cocktail of disappointment and sadness. If they just grew apart there will be a range of emotions around "what could I have done to prevent this" and in all cases, if there are children there will be sadness for them.

And in most cases there will be financial issues that permeate the energy of a new relationship. It is on the record that men suffer hugely from divorce in financial terms. My friend Dan lost 80% of his wealth and the divorce cost him $80,000 of what he had left. This is not an empowering place to start a new relationship and it's very common. There are many men out there who are decimated by the financial cost of divorce and who have given up on ever really having a live-in committed relationship again. It's for you to decide how viable a potential relationship is. There are always successes and the relationship is not about his money but what you can create together so you just need to be sensible about whether it can work for you or not.

Another problem with Mr Just Out with Kids is that he will do everything to see as much of them as he can and you will be ditched on a moment's notice if there is a possibility to see them. Not only will he spend as much time as he can with them, his depleted resources will go into buying stuff for them in lieu of having lots of time with them. That's all part of the guilt trip and his need to maintain a relationship with them, and whilst it's nice that he cares and has a responsibility, he's probably not ready for a relationship with you.

Mr Just Out is joined in this category of unavailable men by Mr Separated. In my expert opinion everyone who is not single is married so Mr Separated is really Mr Still Married and you need to steer very clear of him too. He will no doubt tell you he is over the marriage. And he may well be but you may not know for a while and in that while you may fall madly in love with him......and then find he is totally unavailable emotionally. Not a good scenario!

Relationships that are over usually take a long time to sort out. Sometimes they are never sorted out, and sometimes they to and fro like a yo-yo, on again off again for a very long time. You cannot help in that sorting out process. It is not something than a new woman can do for any man. Sure you can be a diversion but that is like putting the real problem on the back burner only for it to bubble up when you least expect it. Anyway whatever he tells you is based on his biased opinion of the relationship's demise, which is only half the truth at best. Given that he is trying to woo you he is unlikely to say that she threw him out because he had an affair or two, or that he had addictions of some kind or was a bad provider or whatever the reason was. He will spin you a line that may well include "she wouldn't have sex with me" to get you feeling sorry for him. It may well be the truth, but you don't know that he never came home from work sober, do you? Or that he spent all his money gambling in the casino. Or that he screwed dozens of other women. Or whatever the reason was, or whether in fact it is true or not.

So how do you know if this tall dark and wonderful man who's chasing you is really over his marriage or long term relationship? Well the obvious starting place is to look whether the indentation on his finger from his wedding ring is still visible. Mine took a long time to vanish and I guess my finger is no different to thousands of others. That may tell you how many months he's been on his own, or it may not.

What is not so obvious up front is his relationship with his ex. And for a million reasons this is important to know. Not the least reason is that if you want to be the next Mrs, you need to know how he treated her. If it was she that ended the relationship, then you need to watch out for his anger, his resentment and perhaps his willingness to get back to her. If she ended it because he had an affair, then take that as a Red Flag. If he did it to her, it's quite possible that he'll do it to you too. Dee knew about her fiancés ten-year affair during his previous marriage and had even met Susie, the American woman, just before her marriage to Chris. Never thinking the behaviour would be repeated, she was devastated not long into her marriage to learn that Chris was involved with another woman, and then many others before she eventually left him. What is that they say about leopards never changing their spots? So listen to what he says, and believe him. Don't think it happened once and can't happen to you; it can and probably will.

If he's vindictive towards his ex, then at some point he will be vindictive to you too. I always say watch how a man treats a waiter when you are at a restaurant for he's bound to treat you the same way down the track. People's natures do not change. Ever.

Dating you may be an important diversion in his life to ease away the pain of missing his family life, his kids, his financial insecurity and so on. It may be nothing more than that, and that is simply not good enough for you.

Depending on how the relationship is going with the ex you will be able to get a handle on his emotional availability. If he still wants to get back with her clearly he is not available for you. If he is in regular contact with her or is fighting with her, you will know there is still a big emotional investment in the marriage. And pay attention to his version of why the relationship ended. You may find it is a serial trait in him that will impact your relationship as well. For example, if he tells you there is no love in the marriage, it may simply be that he is not able to love and that is a big Red Flag for you too. If he

85

tells you he saw his ex in the shopping centre and turned tail and literally ran in the other direction as Matt told Barbie, his new paramour, trust me that he is still hugely emotionally connected to her and not available for you.

If he has been separated a long time from his wife and is still not divorced, you will want to ask a very big Why? For some it's no doubt a protection, like some girls have affairs with married men so they don't have to commit to them and can still have some dinners paid for and uncommitted sex, some men won't divorce so they can't do something rash like get married again. And some know that they could never afford another wife or committed relationship.

Clearly there are also the Peter Pan's out there who stand firmly in the category of Mr Unavailable. Gorgeous they may be, they have never grown up and are often heavily in their feminine energy. A man who resides in feminine energy is not going to provide the protective safety net we girls want in order to express ourselves fully in our feminine essence. These guys have probably never committed to anything of any consequence in their lives and they have no idea that they must be in their masculine purpose to create a safe space for us to nurture the relationship and to open to loving them fully. These Peter Pan's will want you to do all the organising for them. They will ask you for clues on what you should do together and where you should go. They will probably never take the initiative and book a restaurant or a theatre and tell you to get ready at 7 for a fabulous evening. They're more likely to want to hang out with you, and probably not spend any money on you. And they are likely to have lots of women friends so you may never know how exclusive or not your relationship is. Keep them as friends to go to the movies with if you must but don't invest your emotional future in men who have never, and will never, grow up.

So Peter Pan's are Red Flags no matter how charming they are. They need constant attention and that is both boring and draining. Leave them to girls who don't want a passionate lasting committed relationship full of joy and love or the girls who are happy to do all the do-do-doing just to have man around. They are not real men and don't deserve real women.

Other Red Flags classified as Mr Unavailable are men who have been single for so long that they do not really have anything much to offer you. They are selfish, can be narcissistic or at least self obsessed, too set in their ways and often perfectionists as well. How long is too long varies greatly and it can vary depending on their bank balance. It is well known that men evaluate their ability to get women according to their status in the wealth department. A wealthy man believes he can get more women than a man of moderate wealth; that's why they have themselves photographed on an internet dating site with a fancy car or yacht in the background. So men with less wealth than others feel they have not as much to offer and tend to stay single for much longer. It's bad enough to be rejected, but to be rejected before you start because you can't provide your woman with any of the obvious trappings of success is pretty dismal. It all becomes so obvious when captains of industry not only have mistresses; they are seen out in public with their mistresses and have high-powered legal cases after they have died from the mistresses wanting more money.

Younger clients, in the 20's and 30's tell me the men they meet who have been married have lots of financial problems and as much as they want sex, they don't really feel they are ready for another committed relationship whilst they are not in their own home and have kids to pay for. These guys can well be seen as Mr Economically Unavailable for women wanting a committed relationship.

Older clients - women in their 50's and early 60's - tell me many of their divorced internet dates have had one seriously long relationship since their divorce. These relationships vary from 7 - 12 years, have all been live-in and generally ended by the woman. My clients report that these men are now damaged goods and therefore Mr Unavailable. They are not prepared for a committed relationship, often they don't have the funds to ever own their own home again, they certainly don't see marriage as something they want again and they are pretty lack lustre in many ways. They are certainly not prepared to put out a huge amount of energy to get a woman and most probably don't expect to be in a long term relationship again. So generally speaking they are Red Flags too.

Then there is Mr Unavailable who has a fear of commitment. He could be any age and with any relationship history. He'll often come on strong and then back off so you don't really know where you are with him. He's on the net because he wants a relationship but he is terrified of losing his power and his money so he is not interested in a commitment. He may be captivating and fun, he may have perfected the art of seduction but you will be left wondering when he transfers his attention onto Miss Next because he is getting too close to you. Watch out for him and leave before you get hurt. He won't change.

The thing about Mr Unavailable, in all his forms, is that he is transparent in his unavailability pretty quickly so if any of these characteristics appear early in the peace, you need to decide whether it's what you want or not. If it's too big a compromise, then pack up and leave. Say goodbye nicely and move on to someone who can and is prepared to put effort into creating a beautiful relationship with you that has a viable future.

NOTE TO SELF:

♥   I'll ascertain as quickly as possible how emotionally available he is

♥   I'll err on the side of caution to preserve my emotional wellbeing

♥   I'll leave the Red Flags to others

CHAPTER ELEVEN

MR DESPERATE DAN

Mr Desperate Dan is to be avoided at all cost. He is a Red Flag, a time waster and will advance your project not at all!! Sadly, he lines up in droves on the popular dating sites and either has a very large ego or a very small brain. Or, quite possibly, both.

For starters he has very little on his profile. Lots of the spaces are left blank or he says it doesn't matter who you are. He doesn't care what age you are, he says he doesn't have a preference for whether you live close to him or not, he has no preference about whether you have children or want children, what religion you are or who you vote for, he cares not if your eyes are green, brown, blue or presumably you could be an albino and he wouldn't care. He doesn't even care if you have a quiet introverted personality or are a party lady and he certainly doesn't care what level of education you have or what your job might be.

Now interestingly, all those things are the things you look for when you are looking at the profile of a man who has made contact with you. You want to know these things because they are the things that define whether you want to get to know him or not. Let's say you were quiet and introverted and hated parties, you wouldn't want to be with a party boy. It's so basic, stuff like that, because no matter what, our natures do not change. And if you are looking for a life with someone you want to know that on the basic things you have a good degree of compatibility, don't you?

For you, clarity is power so you'd certainly want to know if he had children, whether they lived with him or whether he wanted any more and what his marital status was, and all the other details. But he doesn't, this man, Mr Desperate Dan, he is not concerned with the details. So in not stating what he wants he is offering himself to all and sundry and one would have to ask him, how would he know if he got what he wanted?

So Mr Desperate Dan does not stipulate what he wants and it's also true to say that he does not really read your profile. Why he doesn't, is that it's meaningless anyway. Let's pretend we are making a cake. Skimming through the list of ingredients, we'd know we need to buy chocolate if we are making a chocolate cake. But if we are making plain cake then chocolate is not of any interest. Same deal with Mr Desperate Dan. He has no idea what his ideal woman mix is so he stipulates nothing. Sometimes he even doesn't care if she is 20 or 40. And the reason he doesn't care is that he doesn't really expect to meet anyone anyway. He's probably had a rather dismal relationship life, has a low self worth and currently, and perhaps for a long time, not much of a life. So he goes on the internet joins a dating site and maybe finds an old photo at a work function or a wedding where he tries unsuccessfully to crop out everyone else.

Sometimes Mr Desperate Dan can be identified because he has no photo which to a self-respecting woman indicates a Red Flag: he is (a) married (b) unattractive (c) has low self esteem (d) doesn't want his friends to know or (e) up himself because he thinks he has an important job and shouldn't have to be on the internet to find a woman. Or he could quality in all of the above.

Mr Desperate Dan has a life that is pretty boring and it's likely he doesn't have a lot of money. And therein lays a big problem. Divorce we know is seriously damaging to most men. They are usually the ones to move out of the family home into some dingy flat, have lost up to 80% of their life savings and are still paying child support. Often they can hardly manage to keep themselves going and their priority is to take the kids out on the weekends to keep a semblance of family connection in their lives.

Relationships to these men are a dream. They tell me that the notion of trying to afford another relationship is just too difficult. But even though they are not in a position to have what they want it doesn't stop them looking around and because they don't expect anything to eventuate they have very fuzzy lines about their requirements. Basically they go for the lowest common denominator, ie they don't care what they want or what sort of a match it is, because they are not really hopeful of having anyone at all.

Tragic, yes. But ladies who want a loving and committed relationship cannot afford to dally long with these men. Harsh? No not really. They want a man with whom they can have an abundant life, and as there are plenty of them out there Mr Desperate Dan and his colleagues aren't really in the race.

Other kinds of Mr Desperate Dan who are not totally desperate financially are desperate in other ways. They have few social skills, they don't believe they deserve a good woman, they have low self worth and for them the internet dating sites (and, sadly, porn sites) fulfil a need that otherwise may not get met. So they surf the sites and send you smiles or winks at random. You may look good, even too good for them but they make contact on the basis that it's a numbers game and by the law of averages, someone must respond positively. Or else they are wired for rejection and they take that in their stride and keep pressing the smile or wink button to a new line up of ladies. They have committed once and it's the biggest and last commitment they will make. For the rest of their lives they will settle for less. If you go along with them, there won't be a lot of upside in the relationship. And if they are looking for a woman between 40 and 65, trust me they will be looking for someone to keep them.

These are the men who often communicate with you late at night and at weekends. Late at night because it is then their minds turn to sex, and weekends because they are not at work and have not much to do. So ladies if you really want a long term committed and loving relationship and you hope you'll find it on the internet, you have been warned to keep away from your computer late at night and at weekends.

Apart from isolating these guys who really can't offer you what you want, it saves you from being tempted to respond to someone who may sound a little more alluring. If do are tempted and you do respond, there are three possible scenarios.

Firstly, he will disappear because he then has to make a choice as to what to do next. On some sites this may mean he has to purchase the right to email you and invite you out. That costs money, as of course does the date, if you get that far. Some disappear at this point especially if they think they can't get easy and cheap sex with you.

The second scenario is that he may invite you out and its odds on you will get offered a coffee. And you will either be bored and wished you were at home with a good book, or you'll get through it and politely say no to a next date (also likely to be a coffee) if he makes it that far. Often they will ask you for another date and you never hear from them again. That's because they don't really know what they want and they are unsure whether you will be able to provide it for them.

The third scenario is available on one popular website where he has the possibility to send you a free note saying "if you send me an email I will buy you the first coffee". Let me tell you men, this is the cheapest and most loathsome response any woman could receive. She has acknowledged your initial communication, read your profile, decided she would like to know you more or meet you and you are so mingy that you won't spend a lousy dollar on an email to her. Well, guys you've heard it now. Not one decent woman I have polled would have anything to do with you if you sent this message. Not one. I know women who have told you how appalling a response it is, that it is cheap and mean and totally unacceptable and you still don't get it! If she looks and reads what you want, and do the right thing that dollar could be the best investment in your life.

And, if by chance, any of you ladies have actually bought into that scenario, shame on you. If he treats you so dishonourably and meanly and cheaply before he has met you, trust me, that mean streak is there.... firmly entrenched in his DNA and it is there for the long haul. Haven't you heard the saying mean of pocket, mean of spirit? It's true so do nothing, don't even respond and delete him from your list. I don't care how little or how much money he has, that is a despicable way to approach a lady and deserves a resounding silence from a lady wanting a real relationship.

Other Mr Desperate Dans, if they get to the email communication, want to elongate the conversation rather than arrange a date. That makes no sense for a lady who wants a real relationship, and now. Women who want to give and receive love don't want to spend hours or days or weeks or months communicating with a man who is not able to be in a relationship however much he fantasises about it. Some of these Desperate Dan's have a habit of trying to hook you in by this lengthy communication, but there is no point in discussing every aspect of your life with anyone you will probably never meet when you could be out there meeting someone who is suitable. There is a time to move into real time, not cyber time. If he hasn't asked you for a date by email 3 or 4 at the latest, move on. If you think the only way you'll get a date is to ask him for one, then you need to go back to basics and learn about hunters and the hunted. Contacting him does nothing but advertise your availability. When you're scarce he may be interested, all men, not just Mr Desperate Dan, but when you're available then he loses interest fast.

I feel for the Mr Desperate Dans of this world but my clients want a functional relationship; they want someone who is able to love them and with whom they can create a great relationship. What they are really saying is that they want someone to recognise them for their uniqueness and to love them for that, for the long haul.

These women spend time and effort creating a profile that shows the world who they are. When a man who has no preferences and no priorities makes contact with them it diminishes the whole deal. They want to be recognised for their specialness and who they are, not have what they want totally ignored. These women are not at a pub or a bar where all that matters is their looks; they have made themselves vulnerable by taking the time to write a little about who they are and what they want. At least they want to be acknowledged for that and for the men out there to read their profiles and respond because some of the things in those profiles actually set alight a spark of something in that man. That is our reality, men, and we want you to honour us for that.

During my research I put up a phony profile on a dating service for about a week that was very explicit about what I wanted. It had 12 items that I absolutely must have in a partner with a note saying please don't reply unless you genuinely can offer these things.

This was the list.

1. He is emotionally and legally available and committed to emotional intimacy.

2. He is deeply passionate and sensual.

3. He is highly intelligent, engaged with life and open to constant learning.

4. He lives in strong masculine energy and is a strong decision maker.

5. He lives a lifestyle and has a belief of health and vitality.

6. He has a track record of success and measurable wealth and abundance and is very generous.

7. He is a brilliant communicator and has a social personality.

8. He is a man of truth and integrity, honesty and honour.

9. He is deeply committed to creating and maintaining an outstanding life with me.

10. What he is currently doing is the juiciest thing on the planet for him.

11. He is refined, cultured and beautifully dressed.

12. He is totally willing to support my endeavours and magnificence and will do whatever it takes to adore me and create ongoing romance and beauty in our marriage.

Well, no surprises. Lots of responses and not one of them went within a bull's roar of my wish list. And that's without even exchanging one email or one latte. Granted that some of my requirements could not be fully ascertained by looking at their profiles, the quality of the profiles that turned up was so abysmal that I would not have wanted to go further with any of them. Quite frankly, it was absolutely clear that none of them had read my request at all, or if they had, they were a collection of Desperate Dans.

Ladies, there are plenty of great men out there. When you identify a Mr Desperate Dan, Red Flag him and move on.

NOTE TO SELF:

- ♥ **I will get very well acquainted with Desperate Dan's characteristics**

- ♥ **I'll list the DD's I've known and celebrate they are not in my life**

- ♥ **If he shows up I'll decide to move on**

CHAPTER TWELVE

MR SEX ONLY

Sex is wonderful. It can have so many moods; fun, frivolous, sensual, passionate and breathtakingly beautiful. But before we get between the sheets, women want to feel safe, we want to feel desired for who we are, we want to feel ready for it and we want to feel that our man is not having sex with anyone else.

Some of the sexual predators on the internet dating sites are married but I am certain that there are a vast number who are not: just lazy guys who haven't the social skills to get a good woman and think they have the sexual skills to get a good lay.

Whilst these men obviously have lots of success in the bedroom, they don't appeal to decent women who are seeking a permanent and committed relationship. We all know that men are predominately visual and get turned by by a vision on their computer and that women need to feel; something which rarely happens via their computer screen. Ladies are aroused into sexual activity by someone they meet who turns them on.

It's true that men pick up women in bars and pubs and that some women do the same with men. Fuelled by alcohol, maybe a dare or two and an injection of hormones, sex between two relative strangers who perhaps don't even know each other's names is commonplace. For both men and women free and casual sex is easy to get, certainly any night of the week in a big city.

So when women go to a dating site they are there to find a partner: a man to love, perhaps to marry, to have children with and grow old with. Whilst you will always find some that do have sex with a lot of the men, the ones who are my clients do not go there to find a man to have sex with without the rest of the package.

It was not into my ear you whispered, but into my heart. It was not my lips you kissed, but my soul.   Judy Garland

For some men, however, dating sites are seen as a perfect pick up place that saves them time and money they don't have to spend doing the round of singles clubs and bars. And they must have some success or else they would not stay on regular dating sites, but would move instead to those expressly for sex. Some of these men are very skilful in the seduction department, so skilful that good women don't even understand where he is going with his questions. For example, when he asks where you live, he is probably ascertaining how far away you are and can he get sex without a lot of effort. When he

102

asks what you are on the site for, he is hoping you will give an answer that will indicate you want casual sex. When he asks if you like exercise, he will be hoping you are a black belt holder in horizontal folk dancing. How have you found the site is shorthand for how many men have you met and how available are you? If you say heaps, or you have been on it for a long time, then he will assume you have been available for casual sex and still are.

Everything Mr Sex Only does is testing you for sex...it is all testing your backbone and how quickly you will cave in. If he doesn't get a clue from you first up he will ask you for coffee, and if that looks promising he will progress it to a drink thinking that a cocktail or two is a sure fire way to get into your knickers. If he asks you for dinner and says he'll pay he wants instant rewards in your bedroom that night.

Mr Sex Only will certainly turn the conversation to sex chat, and if you find that uncomfortable, then its time you left with a Red Flag in your hand. Most ladies don't know how to deal with this and play along with it, not wanting to be seen as a prude. But men are so adept at crossing the line that you can be involved in this conversation before you know it. They are a lot smarter than most of us because it's a skill they have worked on. He'll break physical barriers by touching you on the arm or on the knee too, way before you want him to.

> **Never be afraid to leave, the universe always has a back-up plan.   Dr Buzz McCarthy**

Obviously Mr Sex Only's persistent use of blatant sexual conversation brings many rewards to them and clearly there are women out there for whom it works. But amongst my clients and ladies who have attended my workshops, I have never had any one admit to welcoming sexual innuendo from unknown or little known men who contact them via internet dating sites.

Some have shared stories of men sending web cam shots of themselves masturbating, asking if you will do the same, or telling you they have RSI for masturbating so often and could you please help, or showing you photos of him feeling up a woman to turn you on and these good women are horrified. But this is the reality of genuine dating sites. If the conversation goes to adult dating sites where there are explicit sexual requests for a wide range of options most ladies find degrading they are completely put off internet dating.

When Sarah, a nurse in her late 20's, was contacted by Mike, she thought he looked OK and agreed to a further communication. Like all women, she hoped he had read her profile and at least acknowledged what she wants in a mate before he made contact with her. But when she received his email she realised he either had not read anything about her or was completely disinterested in what she wanted. For it was all about him. She sent me his email and for those of you who maybe do not believe this sort of thing happens, his communication is here in its entirety, poor spelling and punctuation and all!

"Hi, I liked your photos and profile that's why I'm contacting you. I'm looking for a lady like you who would like exciting sexual times with a older man, I'll treat you with respect, If you are interested please read on.... I desire sensual, erotic, intoxicating sexual pleasure. And if you have a SOFT TEASING TOUCH and want to eagerly explore me with pure unadulterated sensual passion... for hours, and you want to be explored the same way and love cuddles and kisses.... I can be yours! I am looking for one (1) woman that I can enjoy spending casual time with.... But mainly enjoying one another's company in the bedroom. I'm not after anything serious at this stage in my life, but If your fun, have a sense of adventure and don't mind trying new things. You may just have my interest! And yes I am 100% straight.... And drug free and healthy. If You Would Like to Meet Somewhere for A Drink, A Coffee? We Can See One Another and See What We Think...It's Up to You! Yes, total discretion at all times! If you're not interested, please reply back that's the polite thing to do. Right? Cheers! Please contact me somehow...... If you can, please message me back. Or email me" (and he gave his private email address here).

Sarah was shocked. She had never received such a blatant and disgusting communication in her life. An experienced woman would be horrified. A not so worldly woman would be frightened. This is one of the things that make good women nervous about internet dating. Not just receiving an email like this, but "what if the man I am about to meet for a coffee is like this too." And how will I know?

Women don't always know. Because you like to think of everyone as decent and because Mr Sex Only is so skilled he can sneak up on you and put you in an uncomfortable situation before you know it. Many young women have not been faced with this sort of scenario and older women out of a marriage already hurt or disappointed by a man they put their trust in are horrified that there are men out there who are prepared to have sex with absolutely anyone who is available. So the deal is ladies, if you want a lasting relationship, don't be available unless the sex you have is an emotional act of love, intimacy and meaning. Even men will tell you that if you start things with a man at a casual and purely physical level it will never lead to something more meaningful and long-term because men don't work this way.

So here are some suggestions to deal with Mr Sex Only - don't buy into feisty conversation; definitely don't make yourself available on a web cam and be aware of how they try to strip the boundaries off you early in the peace, often trying to make any taboo subject OK before you know what they are doing. If he is chatting you up without a suggestion of dating, there's a big chance that all he wants is casual sex. If you don't oblige or you don't even recognise what he is trying to do, he is skilled enough to know you will probably say no and he will move on without you knowing why. If you don't come across as someone who will have immediate sex with him Mr Sex Only will move on to find someone who will.

Life is complicated enough without getting tied up sexually and emotionally with men who don't really care who you are or what you stand for. As I have said earlier and will say again, women are the ones to create the emotional ambience or the flavour of a relationship, to set the scene and protect themselves from anything but light and goodness so it's up to you to set their standards and not lower the bar, for anything.

And yet the sexual invitation comes via internet dating sites probably more often than you and I realise. These less than adequate men who are not up for a real relationship but want frequent and free sex, without, as Mike says "anything serious at this stage in my life" are repulsive and unwanted by any decent and self respecting woman.

Another client, Dana, an account executive with her own business in her mid 30's, told me of a meeting she had with Thomas, a man who contacted her via a dating site. They shared a couple of emails before he invited her out and they agreed to meet at a well-known coffee shop one Friday afternoon. She thought he looked OK, just OK, but it was not an OK date at all. When he eventually arrived, late because of traffic, the coffee shop was closing so he offered her a drink in a local bar and because it was a nice sunny afternoon and the end of the week, she agreed. What was promised as a 5-minute ride around the corner turned out to be a 45-minute ride to a pub far from her home. What she didn't realise until he said 'why don't we pick up a couple of bottles and relax on my terrace', was that it was around the corner from his home and it was there he had in mind to go, not the pub.

Dana was furious she had agreed to go with him and sit in his dirty little car and listen to inappropriately suggestive comments. She didn't even want to have one drink with Thomas but to be polite she agreed to a quick glass of wine in the crowded terrace bar and she couldn't wait to leave. Even that quick glass of wine was most unpleasant. Whilst the wine was OK the conversation turned to sex and masturbation and things she did not want to talk about with him, then or ever. Clearly he thought that she would be turned on by him talking about these things but in actual fact she was repulsed and couldn't wait to get away, never wanting to hear from him again. Alas that was not so, he texted her with some information he assumed she wanted which she politely thanked him for only to receive an unpleasant text message a couple of days later "not even a thks for my text maybe book yourself into a relationship course you shaw (sic) need it baby thomas".

Some Mr Sex Only men have a little more finesse but the outcome is the same: they don't read their women, want sex without caring who with and try all sorts of devious methods to get it. These men are too fearful to love, they don't want or have given up on the idea of having a proper relationship, they have no balance in their lives and they just solicit sex through the internet. Sadly, they can become spoiled by the women who are out there and too available. These women probably start out wanting a good relationship but give up on it, hoping that they might get a man through sex. That will never happen. They never get to have a proper relationship, only a lot of empty sex with men who never say "I want to be in a relationship". All they say is I was to have some fun. But it's not fun for good women or for women in their mid to late 30's for whom the baby story is uppermost in their minds and of whom men are frightened for that very reason.

Some of these men are also a bit kinky. Melanie, a teacher in her mid 30's was harassed by a Mr Sex Only; a personal trainer in his 20's who asked if she could leave her nightie in her mailbox so he could pick it up. She also told me of contact with a 24-year-old man who asked her if she could help him lose his virginity and of the number of experiences she and her friends had had with men tell them they want kids with the expectation that the woman will melt and give them instant and free sex.

Kathy, a PA of 40, dating again after divorce, met Jeff, a company executive, on the internet and after an introductory coffee meeting agreed to have dinner with him. Meeting in the bar of a city hotel they enjoyed a couple of drinks before he announced he had left his specs in his room. Declaring he needed them to read the dinner menu he asked if Kathy would accompany him upstairs to get them. She declined but he insisted it was quite proper and that he'd be happy if she stood at the door of his room whilst he went inside. Once up there he implored her to come inside and look at the spectacular view along the river. Kathy still declined, knowing that if she put her foot in the door he would put the hard word on her and escape would be challenging. Having no intention of being put in that position she politely farewelled him and went home to a toasted sandwich.

Good on Kathy and good on all the women who know what they want in a relationship and are prepared to hang out for it. There are too many Mr Sex Only's out there, many of whom are initially hard to pick so skilled are they at their art. But no matter how skilled they might be at the act of sex, for most women the act of sex also involves their heart. For them sex without heart is empty and pointless. They want to make love with the right person and that's what they are hanging out for.

NOTE TO SELF:

♥   **I will learn the shorthand they use to see how sexually available I am**

♥   **I am never too shy to leave a date that is inappropriate**

♥   **I am happy to wait to enjoy sex with my special man**

CHAPTER THIRTEEN

MR CHEATER

In a nice uncomplicated world those who register their interest on a dating site should be single, emotionally available for a relationship and truthful. Sadly, this is fantasy not reality. Married men or men in relationships proliferate on dating sites and for women who want a committed relationship they must always be a Red Flag. Some are easy to detect; they are blatant enough to say they are married or in a relationship and want a dalliance. And I dare say some are rewarded by their honesty. But the kinds of women for whom I have written this book are good decent ladies who want a permanent loving relationship with an honourable man who wants to commit to them and the relationship.

Whilst some cheating men are quite skilled at the dating game, others are too difficult to detect. A giveaway is their reluctance to give their phone numbers out, or divulge where they work or where they live. Or if they tell you one thing this week and a different thing next week or they tell you not to ring them at home and think that it won't arouse suspicion. For some of them are indeed not very bright and can't remember what line they have given you. I'm told it says in the Koran that it takes 14 lies to cover up one. You know, you can't remember what you told to whom so you make up another story to cover it up, and so it goes on and on. And it's pretty obvious when he can't take you out on weekends or at nights and has to book a hotel for sex that he is unavailable. Amongst Mr Cheater's favourite lines are that his marriage no longer has any passion; his wife is not interested in sex, that he has not had sex for years and that he is staying until the last child leaves high school. Now that's a tempting offer for some.....if only I can offer all this, he'll be free in a few years and I'll have him for myself.

If you tell the truth you don't have to remember anything.
Mark Twain

Not true. Whilst some men do leave their wives for The Other Woman, often The Other Woman is not what they want in a long term partner and even if they leave their wife they will choose another partner instead of The Other Woman.

Dating a married or cheating man is like driving down a road full of potholes. You go along for a time with everything hunky-dory, then off you go down a pothole - either physically or emotionally. You'll want him on your birthday. Sorry ladies, if it's a Saturday or a Sunday or a Holiday or an evening, he's busy at home. He may get time to have roses delivered, but he won't bring them to you himself. You'll not have him for your holidays either, nor at the big celebrations like Thanksgiving or Christmas or Easter. He's with the family; his family and his wife, the one he vowed to love for better or for worse. And better or worse it may be for him, but it's always worse for you. For not only do you not get to share ordinary things with your man, the time you spend with him and energy you exert planning a life with him will completely take you out of the energy of dating other men who could provide you with the lot. Mr Married Cheater is Mr Red Flag.

Michelle, a brilliant writer, well travelled and with her own business, met Simon on the internet whom she had briefly dated when they were at high school and at university. By the time she met him again, she was living interstate and he was well and truly married with two daughters and running a well-known company. She was captivated by Simon and fantasised about why they had not got it together way back then and how they could now. Every time Simon visited her town they had steamy sex and she planned and schemed to have a future with him. A highly intelligent woman, with a son she chose to have out of wedlock, she arranged her life to be with Simon when he was in town. And he was in town a lot, but not always with her. A close girlfriend called her one morning to say "I bet you had a great night last night?" And when she asked why she was told "I saw Simon at your favourite bar and I presumed he was waiting for you". Not only was he not waiting for her, he had not even phoned her. But plan she did, believing that he would leave his wife and happily let go of his prestigious position and millions of dollars just for her. Sadly, this never happened, Michelle developed liver cancer and died in her early 50's, a great woman gone too soon. Simon still has his family, his property and his millions and probably a girl in every town too. She was important to him, that I know, but not important enough to lose the lot for.

Mr Cheater is a title not exclusive to men who are married. There are plenty of guys out there whose girlfriends think they are in committed relationships that are not just available but actively seeking extra-curricular relationships. The deal is the same. If he's sleeping with another woman all or most of the time he's not available for a woman who wants a committed relationship. And if he cheats on her and you win him, guess who he'll cheat on next? That's a given!

> **Honesty: if you don't have it, it doesn't matter what else you have. Dr Buzz McCarthy**

We live in times of immediate gratification. We all do stuff with little regard to the consequences. We live fast and we play fast but if you fall in love with a married man in the expectation that he will leave his wife for you, you are likely to be disappointed. Committed relationships should be based on love, respect, trust, integrity, loyalty, support and a shared vision of the future. Marriages have the additional component of fidelity built into their vows. Yet statistically 30% of women and 45% of men have a sexual dalliance with someone else during the life of their primary relationship.

What constitutes a sexual dalliance probably depends on who you are having the conversation with. However, there is no doubt that in recent years the goalposts have shifted radically. Whilst in the past sexual intercourse with someone not your spouse was "it", nowadays there is a Pandora's Box of sexual delights that could be considered an affair. It all depends on who is making the call. If Jack is regularly lunching with Maggie but fails to tell his wife or girlfriend, is he having an affair? He may or may not be groping her under the table and wishing he could fuck her or he may be sending lots of suggestive texts, but do all of these things mean an affair?

Did Bill Clinton rewrite the rule book on what breaches the matrimonial contract with the infamous statement that his oral sex with Monica did not constitute infidelity?

The internet has made easier the path of an accidental affair. Social media sites, where people can check out former or potential lovers, are rife with tantalising suggestion and even with no actual touch emotional infidelities are increasingly an issue as intense exchanges of sexual energy are played out on line. And of course they also flourish in the hot and steamy arena of text messages. Technology means we are more connected and effectively broadens the definitions of infidelity. There is no longer agreement on what constitutes an affair. It is a grey area and has many interpretations. Is it physical contact or is it flirtation or is it contacting your ex's on Facebook? What is harmless and what crosses the line is the big question.

For me it is the intention that counts and if you are open to your flirty texts leading somewhere then you are committing a breach of trust. You may not have sex with the recipient of the text messages but if you think it's a possibility and you are leaking sexual energy that rightly belongs within your committed relationship then you are having an affair. In this instance emotional connection equals physical connection whether it stays in cyberspace or not!

The number one Red Flag is the knowledge that affairs constitute a breach of trust. So if you come across a Mr Cheater who is married or in a committed relationship and wants to have sex with you, assume that he lacks the basic qualities you want in a mate, such as integrity, honour and trustworthiness.

> **Trust is like a vase, though you can fix it, it will never be the same.   Dr Buzz McCarthy**

For Mr Cheater, "I'm up for having a dalliance on the net" is clearly ok about being dishonest. He has no regard for his marriage or his wife or partner and if push comes to shove, he has no real regard for you either. You might think you are his Numero Uno, but you are not. When you are in a relationship with someone who is committed to someone else, he has only one foot in your dalliance, and he has the other foot firmly out of bounds to you - tied up with his mortgage, his kids' school fees, his wedding ring, his parents-in-law and all the rest.

If you are on a dating site, it is almost certain that you will be contacted by a Mr Cheater. Often he won't spell out in any detail what he wants in a woman - that is a clue. Sometimes he'll be blatant enough to say that he is married or in a relationship. Often he won't post a photo in case he is recognised. Sometimes he'll try to cover up his relationship status so you need to ask the questions to uncover his subterfuge as quickly as possible. It's not difficult; you just have to be alert.

There are plenty of sex and cheating-only sites available with increasing memberships. He's not very smart if he doesn't find them and join up. But you need to be smart. You need to recognise the characteristics of Mr Cheater and you need to be committed to preserving your well being and your vision of a loving man who is only committed to you. Let the others go. Don't go there. It's a no win situation. Red Flag all those who appear to be Cheaters and move on.

NOTE TO SELF:

♥   I am aware that Mr Cheater uses genuine dating sites

♥   I will have nothing to do with married or cheating men

♥   I won't get caught up in someone else's dishonesty

CHAPTER FOURTEEN

MR ADDICT

People with addictions are not easy to be in relationship with. No matter what form their addiction takes, someone with an addiction will make something or someone more important than you. And that is not a good place to start or maintain the sort of loving relationship that will rock your socks off.

A truly loving relationship is one where two people open their hearts and souls to one another and make a commitment to be and give everything to their partner and the relationship. That's not just in an ideal world, it's what we all desire and it's what we should all expect to be possible. Life has its rocky roads and relationships certainly have more than their fair share of challenges so to form an intimate relationship where your partner has an addiction makes the road rocky from day one. Only a serial rescuer would want that and it would not be much joy for her in the long run.

When there is an addiction in the mix, he is really not available and this creates a huge stumbling block to a sustainable relationship. What form the addiction takes is irrelevant. It can be any one of a number of things, alcohol, gambling, sex or drugs and the outcome is the same.

Depression is another and the statistics on men using porn would indicate an addiction with rapidly growing numbers.

Megan, a real estate agent in her 30's, met Brian on the internet and they started to date and enjoy each other's company. He seemed pretty normal, had a promising career and was good company but he didn't seem overly interested in sex. Megan hadn't had a guy for a while and as her interest grew she wanted to have sex with him. A couple of romantic sessions in her bedroom proved pretty unsatisfactory and she began to wonder if there was a problem with her. No, the problem was Brian. He was addicted to porn sex and admitted reluctantly that he masturbated many times a day to an image on his screen. It is well documented that some porn addicts cannot perform sexually without the stimulation of pornography and that porn addiction may be part of a more extensive sex addiction which means it usually remains very private and stays out of the realm of sexual interaction with others. Clearly Brian had this problem.

Jayne, a personal trainer of 44, had ten years between her first and second marriages and much of that time had been spent reading books and acquiring knowledge on relationships. When she met Mike on line she felt he was very different from Husband No. 1, Danny, and in no time they fell in love and decided to get married. It didn't take long, in fact within only three months of her new marriage she realised she had been attracted to exactly the same kind of man and the alcohol and money issues that made her first marriage impossible had already showed up in her second. Trying for the next four years to make it work whilst he continued to drink and be totally irresponsible with money, she faced an uphill battle where her health and business suffered dramatically. When she finally found the courage to leave Mike she had to pretty much start her career again and was totally disillusioned about her love life.

So what is an addiction and who is likely to become an addict? People who have a dependence on anything at the expense of other aspects of their life are considered to have an addiction. If something interferes with your work, your relationship life, your family life or your social interactions it is a problem. Addictions often run in families. If his father was an alcoholic, the chances are strong that he will be too. If there is one addictive pattern of behaviour, there will be others, for instance if he's an alcoholic he may well also be a gambler. For pain free dating and relationship life, you must Red Flag anyone with an addiction.... whether it is porn, gambling, alcohol, depression, drugs, sex or anything else that indicates this person is not really available to you.

Sadly, they are often not really available to themselves either and the worst thing you can do is to think you can help them. If they want help, there is a vast number of professionals trained to do just that. Generally, addicts do not either see a need for help or want help and if you buy into their story you become their rescuer, nothing else. If you've done that before you will know how unrewarding it is and how unbalanced the relationship was. It's a definite no-go zone for any woman with standards. Remember being with your lover is supposed to make you feel better ..... if his stuff makes you feel worse, move on.

> **If we all put our problems in a pile and saw each other's I bet you'd happily take your own back.   Dr Buzz McCarthy**

With the proliferation of internet dating sites and matchmaking services and singles activities and with the huge number of singles, divorced, and widowed people looking for relationships, it is possible to meet and date more people in a month than, not too long ago, you would have met in a lifetime. This has led to a new classification of addicts - dating addicts. These are people who are always searching to meet the perfect person. No matter how good their current relationship is, they always feel that there is someone even better out there.

Research indicates that the over 40's man is the most likely to become a dating addict so if you're in your 20's or 30's catch them younger and you'll be safer. Many of these men admit to a dating complex when they were younger but now, with a seemingly endless supply of available women, that translates into their need to meet as many as possible, offering a meagre cup of coffee on the first date. Confusion prevails as to who to invite for a second date, but they are rare: mostly Mr Addict simply creates another inflow of available women and lines up another series of coffee dates. If he settles on one woman it will at best last for a month or two. That's a couple of coffees, a couple of dinners and whether or not sex is involved, he'll move on to see what else is on offer.

Even if he meets someone he really likes, and has a great deal in common with, if he finds that there is one single thing he doesn't like about her it's over for him. This is a hint of the Mr Perfectionist that usually accompanies Mr Addict. It's a familiar scenario: at the end of the first date (coffee naturally), he'll ask you if you would like to see him again and says he'll call, but on reflection over the next couple of days he'll come up with something you said or did he didn't like and whilst he is scanning other women on line, he'll focus on the new offerings and you won't hear from him again. Every woman I know who has used internet dating services has told me stories about this man. He is out there in big numbers. They said they had a really nice time, seemed to get on well, had enough in common to want to see them again and never heard another word.

But no, he sees someone else who could fit his fantasy of the perfect woman and his attention flows to her and creates yet another coffee date in the coming days. He'll find something wonderful about her, but on reflection "there is that flaw and I'll just see if there is anyone else I fancy more on the net this week, or then again there's that art gallery opening on Tuesday and the singles function on Friday so I might meet some more women there". And so it goes on. This guy is a dating addict and will not stop searching, even if he gets himself into a relatively monogamous relationship.

And if you're in a relationship with someone you suspect could be still searching, go on line and look at when they were last on the site. That will give you a big clue and maybe the reason to Red Flag him and move on. Sandy, a Sydney life coach in her 30's, was in what she thought was a permanent relationship with Max, who lived and worked in Adelaide. They had met on line and he'd even talked about marriage with her. She didn't know they had a friend in common until Eliza emailed one night after they had both received a funny email from him. Eliza, single and looking for a relationship asked "Oh I hear Max is coming to Sydney, do you think he's a prospect for me?" Sandy exploded as Max had clearly been propositioning Eliza even though at that very moment he was in Sandy's bed. Max thought it was OK! Even funny.

Double standards exist; there is no doubt of that. If you even think you are in a relationship, you need to have the discussion about taking yourselves off the dating site and come up with an agreement that you both abide by. And ladies, be sensible, check every now and then to see if he is still off line.... you may be surprised and he may be a dating

125

addict even when you think you are in a committed relationship. It does happen; sadly, too often.

Earlier I talked about the kind of women who try and rescue men and I'd like you to imagine a triangle with three points and a word each on those points. Those three words are victim, rescuer and persecutor. And undeniably if you are one, you will be all three. Not necessarily in the same relationship, but if you are a rescuer to a man, you may retaliate to your sister as the persecutor and then become a victim in the office. Those three profiles will show up in your relationships until you decide you will never do them again and learn how to do things differently and condition in a new and empowering pattern of behaviour. You will also see them in the men you date. For a healthy life and relationship get off that triangle and don't date a man who is on it. He is a Red Flag.

So ladies, no rescuing any addicts please. You are bound for disaster. You will never be their No 1, which is where you want to be. His addiction will always be his No. 1 and you will be metaphorically "low man on the totem pole". Stay away; there are good, loving, nice men out there to be in relationship with, to marry and to have kids and a great life with. Addicts need treatment but usually take a path through life of half hearted commitments to everything other than their addictions.

126

NOTE TO SELF

♥   **I am very clear who fits the Mr Addict category**

♥   **I will not date a man I know or feel has an addiction**

♥   **It's not my job to try and rescue him**

CHAPTER FIFTEEN

MR REMOTE

Mr Remote comes on warm and fuzzy when he finds you. He presents as a good or even great communicator. He may even have been a journalist or a writer because he knows how to string a line or two together very well.

He'll often send you long messages about his life and his relationships and what he's done and what he wants. They are quite detailed emails and you'll get his work history and his relationship history. He'll tell you why his relationships/marriages did not work for him and that he's great friends with his ex's, which you probably find comforting. He'll usually tell you about some of his passions, the things he loves doing and some of his friendships. Sometimes he'll tell you about the charity work he does and the contribution he makes to others' lives, all of which seems very attractive to you; it reads like a great package. You want to know he's an all rounder and that his life is not just about himself, and you want to know he can knock out a decent email with proper grammar and spelling and punctuation.

You'll think he's really keen on you because of the number and length of the messages in your in-box from him. They will come all day - morning, noon and night; especially at night when he is at home with nothing to do. Some of these men will email you at weekends because they are at home with nothing to do. But you won't read them until Monday because your weekends are full and busy and interesting and you don't check your dating emails, do you?

Sometimes he will invite you to chat with him, but you'll leave chat rooms for others less savvy and with lower standards than you. You have a life and a job or a mission to get on with and time at your computer doing internet dating should be short, discreet and during business hours only. And because it's in your work time you will respond very briefly because you have work to do. And short responses are what you should do. Whilst you have probably not yet recognised him as Mr Remote, these long emails do not require a long response from you. Your outcome is to meet these men and feel whether there is anything there to pursue. Not to write your life history in impersonal emails to men you may never get to know. For as much as they can hide behind fuzzy photographs and sexy or attractive pseudonyms, they cannot hide behind a real date.

Mr Remote however is a type of man who is not really into dating. He loves the thrill of the chase and he will definitely be chasing a number of women at the same time. If he was a dater he would be a serial dater but instead he's the poorer version of that, just a serial emailer always with a promise, always with a compliment, and well versed in the art of seeking more from you than you want to give. We've all fallen into this trap. Thinking here's a man who's really interested in me...he's giving me so much background information on himself as an invitation for me to write an epic on myself for him. So you can get trapped into writing these long emails deep into the evening when you should be enjoying your friends or reading a good book or sipping champagne in the bath. And there you go; even before you go to bed there is a reply from him. Another lengthy tome but it's time to turn in and read it another time.

The interesting thing is that nowhere in these lengthy pieces dashing through cyberspace is there a hint of an invitation to meet. Nowhere.

> **Lots of people want to ride with you in the limo but what you want is someone who will take the bus with you when the limo breaks down. Oprah Winfrey**

My client Sandra, a bright and fun divorcee of 47, was contacted by a guy called Jeremy. He sounded lovely, highly intelligent, had worked and lived overseas and was actively helping people from Asia who had settled in Australia. He'd had two wives, been divorced twice and said he was looking for a long term relationship again. He had in fact been a journalist and she felt they would know some of the same people from her earlier career life. Jeremy sent email after email, pages long about his life and his passions, and the failed relationships got quite a mention. It seemed he was happy to bare the brutal truth about everything in a very gentle way. And he loved what Sandra sent him. He complimented her on every email she sent; he clearly read them carefully and noted some of the things she said. So she started doing the same for him. At first she had skimmed over his missives wondering if there was anything riveting in them to captivate her heart but when she started really reading them the penny dropped that they were generic letters that had been cut and pasted and undoubtedly sent to many other women too. Reading carefully, she found comments completely unrelated to her emails or to his earlier communications that were quite out of place. Dismayed, she played along with it for a moment and suggested they meet, wondering how Jeremy would handle that. Well, it was the deal breaker she thought it would be.... his next communication told her that he didn't really think she was the woman for him and that he preferred Oriental women.

What a waste of time for them both. They clearly had an attraction for each other, they had an intellect that matched, they were both open about their past relationships and why they didn't work and what they wanted next time, and she thought they would have friends in common. It turned out they did know some of the same people but she only found that out after complaining about him to a close friend who had, as it happened, worked with him.

131

Some Mr Remote's seriously would like to meet you but they never will. He won't meet you even if he wants to because he has been so hurt and damaged by other relationships that the email connection is enough to keep him going.

And there are other Mr Remotes, many of them, who have been so financially impaired by divorce that they simply can't afford women. Men tell me that it is not unusual for them to lose 70% of their life savings by divorce and they still have to pay child support. They also have to set up a new home, remain emotionally afloat, keep working to make ends meet and spend both time and money keeping the relationship going with their kids. For them a romantic dinner is a trip down fantasy lane. Even if they got the courage to ask someone out, even a casual dinner would set them back $100 and that would blow not the week's budget, but the month's. Then if she was not someone he wanted to build a relationship with, not only is it a lost dream but a lost hundred bucks and if it was someone he wanted to pursue, how does he then explain that he can't afford dinner out and that he can cook at her place instead? Most women at the beginning of a relationship want to be spoilt by their new man and want to be seen out and about with him, where they can be admired by others who see them caringly respond to each other. Liz and Graham's first date was lunch but from then on he preferred take-away and television, even on a Saturday night. Assuming it was a money issue, Liz soon realised it was also a habit he'd got as an overseas journalist where he'd spent most evenings in a hotel despatching press reports with room service and the TV on.

Some Mr Remote's keep writing rather than arranging to meet with you because they are communicating with so many women at the same time. Often it is the women who have initiated the correspondence but not always. The men tell me they weigh up the advantages of the women who have given a positive response and then choose the most hopeful ones. It's not that they go into it knowing they will do this; they truly are hopeful of starting something but when the crunch comes they choose to do nothing. I think this is a combination of financial pressures and low self worth and in both cases it's a Red Flag for a woman who wants a real relationship.

Only you are in charge of your happiness.   Dr Buzz McCarthy

The other very annoying habit these Mr Remote's have is that they start a very nice communication where you think you have something of interest ahead and then suddenly they go off line. They can be recognised by when you think it's too good to be true, it probably is.   Jen, a 28-year-old yoga teacher, told me after a really nice chat with Peter over a couple of emails he had talked about wanting to speak to her on the phone. Jen's a smart girl who knows what she wants. She still wants the man to make the first phone contact to show if he is really interested so when he wants to arrange a date she gives him her number. So this is what happened with Peter. He'd talked about calling her and given her his number

133

but sitting at her computer one day she saw him come up wanting to chat. During the email chat he asked when he could call and they agreed on a time in a couple of days. Jen diarised the call for 6pm and waited. And waited. Pete did not call. Not only did Pete not call, his profile vanished from the dating site on the day he was supposed to call. So Jen, attractive, vital and enthusiastic to meet this man was left high and dry. He hadn't called, he had taken himself off the site and she could do nothing or she could get angry and pissed off about men in general and how weak and disappointing they are. And it gets worse: there are men who contact women then go off line within the hour and even before the woman has opened up the email.

What Jen experienced happened to Sarah too. The man she was waiting to date gave her such a string of compliments that she was anticipating their meeting as the possible beginning of something special. They had emailed for a few weeks and spoken twice but in neither conversation did he actually arrange a date, saying well, let's look at our diaries and arrange something next week. Then nothing. He never called again, there were no more emails and when she looked at the site his profile had disappeared too.

Clearly this is a tactic of a Mr Remote. He woos you but doesn't come up with the goods leaving many a good woman left wondering what happened, whether it was something she said, or didn't say or whether something has happened to him.

Well the answer is simple, he cannot offer you anything and you don't need to know why. All you need to do is to move on and find someone who will worship and adore you and want to make a life with you. Mr Remote needs to be Red Flagged as soon as you get a whiff of him. He may sound charming, he will certainly appear attentive and he's probably flattering but he will never give you what you want. Remoteness suits him for lots of reasons and relationships are a fantasy. Perhaps he's been hurt too many times, perhaps he doesn't have enough money to really create a new relationship, perhaps he's got a club foot or hair lip, who knows and you don't need to. If any man you communicate with on an internet dating site does not want to meet you within 3 - 4 emails you need to move on and find someone who does.

NOTE TO SELF:

♥   **I will learn to identify Mr Remote at a glance**

♥   **If he blows hot and cold I will leave immediately**

♥   **If there is no date arranged by email 4, I'll move on**

CHAPTER SIXTEEN

MR CYBER FREAK

Whilst opportunities abound in daily life to lie, the internet has provided considerable help for those deliberately deciding to stretch the truth in their relationships. There are websites for those wanting to cheat on their partners anonymously instead of wasting time chatting up a bird in the nearest bar that may or may not come across and might cause trouble to their wife or steady girlfriend. One such website, disclosing a worldwide membership of 6.5 million, offers money-back guarantees if your affair is not memorable. One can only wonder about the criteria and how much fun it would be to read some of the applications.

If you are having an affair and you don't want to be found out, there is a growth of lucrative services you can access through the internet which provide perfect alibis. For a dollar investment you can keep your spouse happy with appropriate noises such as the sounds of a business conference drowning out your calls to her and the kids when you are really on a beach with your lover or tucked up in a motel somewhere with a bottle of French bubbly.

Inauthentic people can and do easily hide behind the veil of the internet

Inauthentic people can and do easily hide behind the veil of the internet. There is little more anonymous than an email sent via a dating site. It carries none of your regular sign-off details like profession or company or phone number and it of course does not disclose your regular email name, service provider or recent photo. Some men actually state that they are married and simply looking for a dalliance and I guess they get results otherwise they would not remain on the genuine dating sites as there are numerous sites just catering for extra-marital encounters.

Mr Cyber Freak comes in many guises. He could well be emotionally unavailable and he could be financially unavailable. I've mentioned these men before: there are a lot of them too financially damaged from divorce to really offer a woman anything much in the way of a relationship. It doesn't stop them wanting one so they go onto the internet and have cyber relationships with women who don't understand when to say no and when to move on. Women too often get caught up in the story of these men, so not only do they waste considerable time on them, they spend massive amounts of emotional energy trying to rescue these guys. And if that's not bad enough, sometimes they come to the party financially and rescue them, or try to, that way as well. My client Brenda, a brilliant, clever and resourceful woman who owns a couple of boutiques, met a thrice married man on the internet and in the course of his third divorce he asked her if she would contribute $100,000 to the purchase of his marital house from his soon to be ex-wife so they could live in it. Whilst Brenda was not sure she wanted to invest her life with Ken she was certainly sure she did not want to invest her savings in a house she would never want to live in. She didn't hand over the money and not long after he showed himself to be completely dishonest and she quickly moved on. Not so quickly for Sue a 42-year-old advertising executive who lent Brian $50,000 from her father's inheritance, hoping they would be married, only to find out he was a no-hoper and she moved on, sadly without the $50,000.

Mr Cyber Freak could be a player who is married or in a committed relationship and wanting a bit on the side. Some women have highly developed radar that pick him easily but many don't and it's the ones that don't, often women who are not particularly worldly, that can come a cropper with these men. They are used to trusting everyone, thinking everyone is as decent as them and sometimes it's well down the track before they realise that is not the case. So the tricksters and dishonest men are happily looked after by many an unsuspecting woman, all made possible by the internet.

There are also Peter Pans amongst the cyber freaks; guys who have never grown up and want to be looked after by women who don't know how to get the sort of relationship they want on their terms and are prepared to pander to these namby-pamby men because they show a bit of interest in them. These men hide from real relationships and meeting women on line is a form of voyeurism for them. They are likely to string along a number of women at the same time and then disappear into space, leaving them not knowing what has happened. You can identify them by their reluctance to meet you, their poor relationship history and their neediness.

There are also men out there on the net who qualify for the Mr Cyber Freak category because they are narcissistic and calculating in the affect they know they have on women, to the detriment of the women. These guys are probably good looking and know it, or charismatic in some way but instead of using their natural talents to create an awesome relationship with a wonderful woman, they tease women, give them the come-on, play with the emotions of a number of women at a time, knowing exactly what they are doing with them and without the slightest intention to meet them. They don't meet them because these men are highly dysfunctional and probably can't keep a relationship going anyway. Narcissism is a barrier to giving, which is what relationships are supposed to be about, because it's all about him.

Some Mr Cyber Freaks have been spoilt or indeed ruined by too much attention from too many women. They might be the good looking ones who bare their muscles in their photos as a way to attract women but because they like the variety and the seemingly endless choice they keep the women at a safe distance behind their laptop screen because they don't know how to conduct a real relationship either. Many of them are simply bored and entertaining themselves when they have nothing better to do. They are men who don't appreciate women and are Red Flags to be avoided.

Other examples of Mr Cyber Freak are the incredibly lazy men who think they can put out a few feelers and have the women do all the work. They have told me they don't want to go half way across the city to meet someone yet they would go to the ends of the earth to link up with a fantastic lady whom they are passionate about. Well how are they going to know they are passionate about them if they stay behind the computer screen and don't travel across town to meet her?? Or is it because he wants sex close to home so those geographically challenged are never going to get a look-in? These men tell me that the ones you chase don't really care about meeting up so they wait for the ladies to contact, them make all the arrangements and then they go along with that. Maybe. Or maybe not. One of my clients calls them limp dicks; men who want a relationship but lack conviction and are unprepared to do the right thing to get a good woman and keep her. Red Flags, all of them.

No matter what his excuse Mr Cyber Freak will be reluctant to meet you. He will want to extend out the internet communication, he will ask you for your personal email address, he will suggest he has a business trip or two coming up and he is not available for a few weeks or he will tell you some other unbelievable story to prevent you finding out who he truly is. The quicker you can find this out, the quicker you can move on which is why I keep saying that if he doesn't invite you to meet him within 3-4 emails, it's time to move on. Anyone can hide behind emails and nothing is more revealing than personal contact. You know that we live in a throw-away society so, with a substantial smorgasbord of partners on offer, why waste time?

Rowena, a fashion designer in her mid 30's who had been internet dating for several years, told me of a fabulous man she was corresponding with and was looking forward to meeting. I asked her when they were catching up and she said, well at this stage they were just getting to know each other via the email and that she was very attracted to Mike and felt he could be the one for her. She then confessed that some of their emails were quite explicit and she was fantasising about some hot sex down the track. When I asked why they hadn't met yet, she didn't really have an answer, other than she kind of wondered too since he lived in the same city. Anyway long story short, they did meet after 3 months of steamy emails and he was an absolute disaster. Boring, unattractive, poorly dressed and with few social skills, Mike had absolutely nothing to offer and Rowena was shocked she had expressed some sexual desires to him when clearly, on meeting, that was the last thing on her mind. Mike had a writing skill and hid behind that and it was obviously not the first time he had chosen to be Mr Cyber Freak. It worked for him but what a waste of time it was for Rowena, an intelligent, attractive, financially secure woman who was seriously looking for a long-term loving relationship. She wasted three months of her life and considerable emotional energy communicating with this boring and unattractive man who could offer her nothing.

So Mr Cyber Freak has finally asked for your mobile number and his email communication to you changes to sms. Yippee!!! You think you've made it??? Well, that would be no. This is just as bad as prolonged email communication, and probably worse. Worse because he knows you will have your phone by your side 24/7 and whilst the quality of the messages will be reduced by sms speak, the quantity can be increased greatly, thus getting your constant attention and pulling in your emotional energy to ultimately no avail. Transition from internet to sms is not progress, trust me. The only progress you can have is sitting down face to face with this man, feeling if you have anything going for each other, and asking questions that elicit each other's passions, dreams and values.

> **Remember that life is perfect right now and that clarity and vision will provide the emotional fuel to get you where you must go.   Dr Buzz McCarthy**

And for that to happen he has to actually use that mobile number and call you to ask you out. It's not difficult to work out how keen he is by the amount of time it takes him to call you once he has your number. If he does it within minutes, at least you've got a man who's able to confront his fears of rejection. If he takes a long time, you have to wonder if he's really interested or perhaps he has no one else on the go and might as well take a chance with you. And of course he might not call at all and that's because as Mr Cyber Freak he has nothing to offer you and prefers to hide behind his computer and his screen name. Never call him, pretending your phone has been out of order or you've been in a meeting all day. He's not worth you doing any work on. It's his job to go to the end of the earth to find you. If he's got your phone number and he doesn't call, he's a Red Flag. Move on.

If he does call and you don't like the sound of him, don't feel obliged to make a date. Countless women have told me they've felt obliged once he has called them to turn up to a meeting and within 20 seconds of the latte being ordered wished they were at home on their own with a good book or a glass of red. Just because he finally calls you do not have to say yes. If he has the sort of voice you couldn't live with for ever then say no. It's not difficult, and it makes good sense not to go out with someone you don't know when you do know you're not interested in him.

Mr Cyber Freak is much happier texting than speaking but if he texts you for a date, leave it a while and text back saying you would rather speak with him to arrange meeting up. You have to make him work for you or else the relationship will always be disappointing. You have to love you more than you love him.... now and for the duration of the relationship to make it work. Trust me on that! And if he doesn't ring do nothing; move on and wait until the next encounter. It is not your job to arrange the date with this man or any man who hides behind the anonymity of cyberspace. And remember that if a relationship starts by text, then one day it will end by text which will be disappointing, frustrating, sad and horrible.

We can have our work done in foreign countries these days by people we don't know for outrageously small sums of money, we don't have to visit our bank to transact all our financial affairs, we don't even have to go out to order our food any more but we do still want real relationships. Cyber relationships are not real. They cannot be and they never will be. Real relationships happen when you can look into someone's eyes, see their soul and their flaws and still decide to stay. Isn't that we all want? Real relationships are out in the open, where we share our lover with our friends, family, workmates and kids. Anyone you can't be seen in public with is someone you should not be in a relationship with. And anyone who wants to conduct a relationship with you via the internet or a mobile phone without a real commitment to get to know you face to face, breath to breath and heart to heart is not worth wasting a moment of your time on. Once you get a whiff that he is playing with you, fobbing you off, creating stories around why you can't meet now, delete him from your computer, your phone, and your mind - just do it before it's too late to delete him from your heart.

144

NOTE TO SELF:

♥ If he wants to keep it in cyber space I will move on and delete him

♥ I don't want a relationship that survives by text messages

♥ I am committed to only spending time with a man I can see and sense in person

CHAPTER SEVENTEEN

MR BLATANT LIAR

One of the great things about being conscious and dating consciously is that you know and accept that not only will he be flawed, but so are you. Yes, we are all imperfect human beings and we are all struggling to have our needs met in life, which is difficult enough, let alone in our relationship life, which for many seems absolutely impossible. For those who have not yet come to that realisation, and for those who see who they are and don't like what they see, the internet provides a safe place for us to reinvent ourselves and to present without flaws. Well, at least that is what we think! But that won't work any more than trying to become a virgin again will work! Once the damage is done, it's done and like Humpty Dumpty, you can't put the pieces back together again.

Nevertheless, the internet is a place for people to hide behind something they don't like or to pretend that they show up without emotional damage. The pretence comes in all forms and is obvious just as much in what we don't say as what we do say. It comes not just when we consciously want to lie about something, it comes because most of us do not see the truth about ourselves let alone acknowledge that baggage is a part of life. It's so much more empowering to meet a prospective new partner and to be focussed on what you can give to each other in the future than stay in the past's baggage.

146

And if he's going to be the one for you, hopefully in your vulnerability you will each allow your baggage to be delved into by the other before you release it and get on with things more important.

On line many people lie to appear more attractive and more desirable. What they don't realise is that if they tell whoppers they will be caught out, usually on the first date, and if they start a relationship on a lie, it will continue that way. Dishonesty in one area of your life usually indicates dishonesty in other areas of your life such as your career; your family life and financial life so profile dishonesty may well open up a can of worms.

> **Whoever is careless with the truth in small matters cannot be trusted with important matters.   Albert Einstein**

My clients report that there are many men out there whose profiles are chock-a-block full of lies. Age is the biggie. There seems to be an unwritten law that you can fudge a few years but some players have a very elastic perception of what's OK.

During the first phone call from 56-year-old "Joie de la vie" with a very blurred photo who identified himself as Marcus, Belinda recognised him as a guy she had known a long time ago. Both thrilled to have reconnected they talked every day

147

for the next few weeks whilst he was travelling on business. They shared some great memories of mutual friends and revealed they had fancied each other and were sorry nothing had come of their earlier association. Marcus invited Belinda to lunch the day after he returned home and whilst she thought they were about the same age she was shocked when she was directed to the table of an old man whose hands shook as he poured the long-awaited celebratory champagne. Remembering him as a good looking dark curly haired man with a sharp mind, she realised that the only thing that remained was the sharp mind. Except that it was now accompanied by a sharp tongue of abuse for when lunch took too long to come and was delivered on a cold plate he insisted they walk out without paying. It turned out that not only was he never Marcus, he was 18 years older than the age he'd put on his profile. No wonder he used a blurred photo! Now whilst a few years seems to be OK and is generally something to be unpacked with mirth on the first date, 18 years seriously indicates a Mr Blatant Liar.

Height is another big one especially for men who are less than around 178 cms. We know from age old research that tall men are generally more respected than short men but what is really respected in life and especially in on-line dating where you are almost hard-wired to lies, is the truth. When Melanie, a 29-year-old hairdresser eventually met an interstate man she had been interested in whose profile said he was almost 6 feet / 1.82 metres (that seems to be a good point men like to aim for) and was barely taller than her 165 cms, she instantly thought less of him even though they went on to have a passionate relationship for a year or so which, surprise surprise ended when he committed a major act of dishonesty.

When Jan's date picked her up in his built up shoes and she squeezed into his tiny car she realised that he wouldn't have been able to see over the steering wheel of anything larger. She might have been able to overlook his height, as she was also short, but Mr Blatant Liar also lied about his age and was actually 75 not the 63 that he's put on his profile.

It's not just the years but it's the lifestyle that goes with it. A man of 63 may well still be having a very busy professional life with a passion and a mission that would appeal to a woman who also wanted that type of life. However most won't still have the same passion or career at 75 and may be spending much of their time chasing a little white ball around on green grass. Now if the woman he contacts is still in a wonderful career that she may not be keen to leave it could create a huge gulf of lifestyle that could not be bridged easily for either of them. So age is not just age, it encompasses lifestyle and mission.

Clearly Marcus was accessing his Mr Blatant Liar status when he posted such an unclear photo hoping that prospective dates would not reject him on the grounds of being too old. I'm told that many men lie with their photograph, not just to fudge the age but to create an image that is false. Caroline, a very good looking landscape gardener in her 20's received a contact from an interstate guy who thought she looked hot, which she felt was an inappropriate term for a first contact. When she opened his profile and saw he was photographed beside a fancy convertible sports car with blacked out number plates, she immediately put him in the Red Flag category. He was saying "look at me, I use Hot language, I look hot (well she didn't think so but presumably he did, in his dark shades), and I'm standing beside an expensive sports car which you need to know is mine and I can buy anything I like, including you". Caroline told me "I felt the Hot intro was tacky, who knows if the car was his and if he's really a nice guy trying to date a nice girl, he didn't need it as a prop." So whilst it was not a blatant lie it did tell a kind of truth that makes many women absolutely not want to meet him. So if it's not yours, whatever the toy is, don't be photographed with it, and if it is yours, allow your women friends to find that out later if they choose to go out with you because they like you not what you have.

For whilst we all want someone with resources to make our lives easier and to have some toys whether they be a nice house or a beach house or holidays abroad or our kids' education, we want the guy not the props. We want to find out who he is. And he is not his props or the size of his bank account especially as women are just as capable of providing all the toys they want these days. We no longer have to rely on our man to buy our toys so if they give us an impression of what they are not it will always backfire.

Other status type things that men lie about are those related to their level of education, the type of job they are in and where they live. Jim was a real estate agent in Perth who had moved to Sydney and done an ancillary health certificate which did not qualify him for the degree in the medical profession which he stated he had on his internet profile. I mean, it is so obvious. If you are a doctor, that's great, but if you are a masseur or a reiki master you are not a medical professional with a degree and any girl worth her salt will uncover that to your detriment on the first date. Or like Mario who presented himself as a photographer and then met Liz at a legal function which he was invited to attend as a therapist. Clearly life as a photographer was a more glamorous option but it didn't do it for Liz and they never dated.

Encouraged by the marriage of friends who had met on a dating site and selected each other on education criteria, recently-divorced Clare, an independent woman of 38, joined up and decided to evaluate her potential dates the same way. Clare, herself a graduate with a higher degree, and a focus on continued learning needed a partner with intelligence and an education that somewhat matched hers. Nevertheless, she found some men who had said they had higher education had in fact barely completed high school. If you know where the goal posts are you can play the game accordingly. If they are a changeable feast you will be disillusioned and disappointed with the man who concocts a story to make him appear more attractive.

Another Mr Blatant Liar had an old Double Bay phone number diverted to his current house in Parramatta to impress. Like what the ......??? Women want to make fair assessments of these men so when you come across the initial deception you immediately ask "what else has he lied about?" and the "what else will I find out about when I'm already in hook, line and sinker?" This is what makes women withdraw time and time again from internet dating sites. My clients are always saying "I'm having a rest from the site for now". It's because they are disillusioned with lack of truth, and disappointed with the number of men out there who are prepared to lie or present themselves in a way that tries unsuccessfully to hide their flaws.

> **I would rather hate you for telling me the truth than love you for telling me lies.   Dr Buzz McCarthy**

Marital status is a very unclear area on most dating sites and leads to a Pandora's Box of deception. For me, single means single, not divorced or widowed. It means never married. But it does not tell you he has been a serial womaniser or the father of 5 kids from 4 women, none of whom he is supporting or whether he had a loving and committed relationship with one woman whom he had never married.

Separated means still married which in my language means he is not available for a woman who wants a committed permanent relationship. And of course there is not a space on any of the forms to tell you how long he has been separated or whether he has a divorce pending or whether he has only got out of a marriage yesterday.... or even that he is not out of a marriage yet......which most of the women I know have encountered. It's called hedging your bets.... if I find someone on the net maybe I might leave her, kind of thing. Mr Blatant Liar and a Red Flag....if you find out soon enough to get out before you get hurt.

Married also means not available and whilst some men do admit to being married on their profile which is a sure indicator there're after sex with no ties, it's not attractive to a woman with standards who wants a committed relationship. Others tick any other box to hook us even when they are married. Divorced is self evident; they were honourable enough to commit to a legal relationship with one woman but we'd like to know up front how long it lasted. If it was 15+ years, it's a different story to 1 or 2 and we'd also like to know just how many divorces they have under their belt before we fall head over heels in love with them. That certainly happened to Libby who was besotted with Stan by the time he had told her he was not very good at the marriage thing, admitting that he'd had three. She tossed it off at the time but when he asked her to marry him and she couldn't imagine telling her friends or family that she was going to be the fourth Mrs. Spencer; she did some really hard logical thinking about his relationship history and left him. Later she told me she'd met Brenda who'd had 8 marriages and it rather put Stan's 3 into perspective. Or not! "If you'd known he'd had three marriages would you have gone out with him

153

once?" And she replied absolutely not, I know we all have baggage but that is too much for me to want to deal with.

So what may not be technically lies, the absence of a place to specify the truth and the emotional availability of prospective partners, leads to serious defects in internet dating profiles. It is true we have a tolerance to lies these days: mostly we accept that car dealers and real estate agents tell lies to close a deal and that politicians, trying to stay in power, tell lies to keep the electorate happy. And most women believe their man would lie about having sex with someone else.

When a person does not live in the truth it can as basic as saying one thing and doing another. Andy a travel agent in her 30's believed Martin when he repeatedly told her the lawyers had his divorce in hand until she discovered the authority papers in his briefcase three months after he'd told her they'd been returned to the lawyer's office. After a marriage to a philanderer, Alison, an advertising executive, had her top boundaries as honesty and integrity. When she met Roger through a dating site and he told her his wife's affair ended their marriage, they declared a mutual boundary around fidelity. Eighteen months later feeling insecure in the relationship over some honesty issues he put himself back on the internet. Not only did he become Mr Blatant Liar but earned the tag Also Not Intelligent because lots of Ali's friends were on the site and she was told immediately he had been seen. She ended the relationship that day and called in her buddies to share the celebratory French champagne. Clearly he didn't learn much about honesty because 6 months later he told another woman he was chatting up that he hadn't been in a relationship for five years. When she asked "so what about Alison?" he scuttled off never to be seen again, without knowing they had mutual friends who knew he had a first class honours degree in lying.

Falling from a great height is always more challenging that climbing up to one so if you know where you stand at the beginning you accept your man's attributes and you work with them. If you think he is something bigger and better than he is, the more disappointed you will feel and the more put off him you will be. When you start seeing the cracks and they don't look good, don't stick around to wonder where else Mr Blatant Liar has lied. Gather up those standards and move on to the possibility of attracting someone more honest and honourable.

NOTE TO SELF:

♥   **I will expect the best but keep my radar on for inconsistencies**

♥   **I will be joyful when he does what he says he will do**

♥   **I live in the truth and expect the same from my partner**

CHAPTER EIGHTEEN

MR PREDATOR

Whilst most of us like to think the best of everyone we meet there are men using dating sites to lead women on and to solicit money. Not quite as obvious as the requests from Dr. So and So at the Nigerian Bank who lets you know that if you send him $10,000 you will be able to access a pile of money in the millions, these men prey on women's emotions until they have them hooked in, and then they ask for money to be wired to them.

Theresa thought she had found a pot of gold when she met Cameron on a poplar dating site. Good looking and very eager to get to know her, on the second communication he asked for her private email so they could email away from the site. He then started plying her with compliments, and, because she was coming out of a very long-term relationship which had gone belly-up, she was extremely vulnerable and easily caught up by his rather overwhelming attention and affection. In hindsight she can't believe how incredibly stupid she was, and although she fell for Cameron hook and line, she kept the sinker afloat and he, in the end may have got her heart for a time, but did not get her funds.

His various profiles list him as either single or widowed, but the one she fell for was widowed and looked serious with glasses; he changes between having no children or children who are not at home, is aged 52 or 55, and in various different industry types and educational levels. Other photos have no glasses and even his eye colour is different in his various on-line profiles but what is the same is his lack of specific requirements for his ideal mate. What rang bells for me was his age preference for a woman ranging from 55 - 67....that always tells me he wants someone more financially successful than him who will pay the bills, but on another of his profiles he said he wanted a woman from 38 - 52. Is he confused or just trying to appeal to many women??? The latter I suspect.

Therese and Cameron started corresponding and when she told him of an artist she'd purchased a small picture from, Cameron responded with the guy's full biography, impressing her, no doubt with the assistance of Google! In their email exchange she suggested a couple of times that they meet but Cameron was always too busy - attending meetings here and there, Melbourne, Sydney, overseas, you name it. Anywhere but where she was so it was always impossible for them to meet. Not only did he go to meetings he gave her an alarming amount of information about each conference, its precise street address, who else attended, what part of the world they represented and what subject matters were addressed; clearly Google to the rescue again, and utterly bewildering for her. More bewildering material, more photos including one of himself with a noted and now deceased Australian wildlife expert, and other photos where he claimed to be part of a

157

global aid team in the Caribbean turned up in Therese's in-box.

But still there was no phone call and his long emails were very boring for a woman seeking love and all about himself until he got to remembering her in his prayers. Whilst some women may well have pulled the plug at this stage, Therese was being hooked in bit by bit and read a dozen times his emails of foreign parts and what he was doing, particularly buying up all sorts of equipment with which to start a new business, and that he was really excited to think of the time they were going to spend with each other "and how much you already mean to me". "But since we are physically separated by miles of emptiness, these expressions and feelings must come in the form of a letter such as this and now I'm blushing...." As if to compensate for the dreariest list of equipment on his shopping list, described in very great detail over many paragraphs he promises to be in touch and sends a poem giving her his heart and soul.

Therese is in seventh heaven. She passes over the equipment list and falls in love even more because of the poem which, when she was telling me her story, utterly nauseated her – as it did me, as an onlooker when I read it. Then, later when she handed over his emails to me she felt unbelievably stupid not to have wondered about his strange descriptions, his use of English which was somewhat odd, "feeling stratified with accomplishing with what I had intended to do" and so on and his New York lunch description which he said was risotto with Porcini mushrooms and then went on to describe braised turnips stuffed with pork!

This diatribe went on and on for weeks, six or seven, before there was any hint of real communication. Ah, just what she had been waiting for: no, not a date, but a phone call - that lasted less than 60 seconds! Whoopee do!!! Then there were 5 or 6 other calls but each was only a minute or two at best. He was always rushed, always arriving or leaving, at airports or meetings and there was never any real conversation. On a couple of occasions when Therese called Cameron she heard click after click after click and felt the calls were being diverted numerous times and usually landing at an answering machine. His emails continued to draw her in, although curiously they rarely commented on anything she had said to him. Even then she sensed that some of his messages were cut and paste jobs because they were out of context. Now she is sure they were.

> **I'm not upset that you lied to me, I'm upset because from now on I can't believe you. Friedrich Nietzsche**

Cameron's geography changed suddenly and she received several pages of emails supposedly from Haiti where he told her he was doing relief work for the United Nations. "I

159

arrived in Haiti a couple of hours ago and already there is so much to be done" but I can't wait to wake up beside you every single day. This email was accompanied by a photo of himself, in uniform complete with guns and with other UN officers on a bus in Haiti. Therese, concerned for his safety, rang the UN who verified that the photo was a genuine UN photo but advised they had no knowledge of the man whose name she gave.

Much later in another email he told her "I don't have any pics in Haiti as I've never been there" and that "the people using my photos are probably Nigerian scanners (sic)" - Therese now is amused that he didn't know how to spell scammers since he clearly was one himself. As for being Nigerian, she listened to his Cockney accent and she was very perplexed about who he really was. But we are getting ahead of ourselves.

Now he's in Dubai and she is frothing at the mouth wanting to set eyes upon this man who sends her "darling" letters telling her she is the most wonderful woman and how loved he feels. Then comes a phone call that makes Therese just a little wary. He is at a function in Dubai (precise street address given) where he is able to buy uncut diamonds with "every last cent on me...but baby I have got some great deals im (sic) sitting on a little gold mine .... if only you can guess where the biggest gem I bought is going to go??????"

With that comes a flight itinerary from a respected Middle Eastern airline where he purports to be travelling in First Class and gives his home address in one of Australia's premier streets and an Australian passport number. Cameron promises to ring Therese before he leaves Dubai because they have arranged to meet at the airport on arrival in Australia and he does this the night before his flight, from a luxury hotel where he is purportedly staying. After a very short chat he passes her over to his Arab-speaking friend who tells her how incredibly lucky she is to have this man who is besotted with her and that he is looking forward to seeing her tomorrow. She doesn't sleep much that night in excitement at meeting this man who has charmed the socks off her but not yet her knickers or her cheque book!

Therese has his flight details, she has packed a little basket of food and she has her heart wide open for this handsome man whom she hopes will treat her better than the one she has been with for the last 20 years. She has put on her glad rags and her favourite perfume and is out at the airport over an hour before the flight is due in. She nervously waits, looking constantly at the arrival monitor, devastated when the flight is delayed an hour. She has a couple of coffees and a nervous pee and waits for this good looking international businessman who is coming home to her with a bag of diamonds.

But Cameron does not arrive on the plane. She waits and waits, expecting him to be first out with the other First Class passengers but there is no sign of him. Her phone rings: this is the moment he has been waiting for and planning for: but it

161

is not the moment she either wanted or expected. Oh Darling, I've been detained in Dubai, I got caught with the stones and they wouldn't let me on the plane. Now I am in the Customs Department and they need money to let me out. Therese draws breath and asks if she can speak to the Customs department to find out what is going on and Cameron tells her there is only one man there who speaks English. You can talk to him. Here is his direct phone number, you can ring it. I'll call you back soon.

In great distress Therese went to her car to cool down and when she arrived home she received another phone call from Cameron who does what he's been leading up to all along this 3-month communication: he puts the hard word on Therese for money. "I've maxed out my credit card buying all those diamonds and I need $6000 to pay a fine to the Customs department so I can leave. Can you please pay it immediately into a Western Union office and I will collect it and be on the flight home to you tomorrow?"

Amateurs built the Ark: professionals built the Titanic.
Dr Buzz McCarthy

Therese had already noticed that the flight itinerary he'd sent her lacked a booking reference number and now that her radar was on high alert she rang the airline to check. Her suspicious were confirmed, they would not issue an itinerary without a reference number so Therese called Cameron in Dubai. "Tell

162

me the reference number of your flight booking and I'll be on the next flight over to help you out" she said. Cameron went silent. Deeply silent. Not a word was said for a minute or so. Then with resignation he said "Oh I suppose I'll have to be a man then and deal with it myself".

End of story. End of communication. Therese heard no more word of love and money from Cameron.

But more was heard of Cameron.

Therese called the United Nations office in Canberra and was told that the same story had been spun to two other women who had contacted them. Both had sent funds to this man. Both were left empty handed and in his words "scanned" ie scammed!

Cameron emailed Therese a month or so later saying he had enough women to meet at present and that he was overwhelmed, but please be on the lookout for some newspaper coverage of this man who had taken my photos and has ripped so many people off, and please send me any photos and contact details he's sent you so I can forward them on to the investigators.

But the story does not end there.

As the universe would have it, a few months after her episode with Mr Predator and his diamonds she heard the story of two women who were waiting at the same Australian airport for the same flight from Dubai for the same man, neither of whom they had met.

Sound familiar?? Well how strange that they got talking. Or is it? When one said "I'm waiting for someone I have never met" the other said "me too" and they started swapping details. The plane arrived. No-one either of them recognised came off and one phone rang. He hardly had the chance to do his usual spiel because she went off at him with such anger and fury that he hung up, the two women were left licking their wounds and went home romance-less but at least not penniless.

The dating site was advised of his shenanigans, the Australian Federal Police was too and neither was prepared to do anything. Mr Predator is probably on the site under another alias, he goes off-line a lot but he still appears in their top 100 males .... which means he is having an awful lot of contact with a lot of women.

As for Therese, she realises she had a lucky escape. Whilst she may not have had the love affair of her life, she did keep her dollars and she is uber cautious now as she continues to date over the internet. She believes Cameron or whatever his name is, operates with a number of other men around the world on this scam. Many of her messages and his on-line profile had cut and paste similarities which she later recognised as a pattern. The huge detail he gave on many occasions as to where he was and with whom, would have been readily available on the internet, and his bleatings about how challenging everything was in Haiti were pure lies; even he stated, later, that he has never been in Haiti.

So ladies, there are people on the internet who are not who they say they are. Their profiles are bullshit, their photos are of someone else and their stories are designed to capture your heart first and then your money. If you stick to all the guidelines, I have given you in the chapters on the men you want to avoid then you will be fine and you will have the ability to really enjoy dating men via the internet.

And there is Mr Right out there too. So read on and see how you can be found by him and enjoy the relationship you deeply desire.

NOTE TO SELF:

- ♥   I am committed to being smarter than I have been before in dating

- ♥   I am keeping my heart for someone that deserves me

- ♥   Never ever will I give my hard-earned money to a man I am dating

CHAPTER NINETEEN

IS HE A KEEPER?

One of the ways we evaluate our world are our values; they determine the experiences we choose, the things we do and the reactions we have. They are our emotional states: how we feel and why we feel. They are the things we want either most or least in our life and they are the standards by which we measure and judge the quality of our relationships.

Most of us are unconscious of our values; we just know whether it feels right or not. They do shift from time to time so if suddenly you were diagnosed with a serious illness, your health would jump to the top of your values list. If you had a financial disaster, then creating financial certainty would jump to the top. If you are not in a relationship and you want to be in one, then relationships are at or on the top of your list. So the truth is your values are determined by what you feel is most missing in your life.

Everything you do in your life will go to satisfying those values, and there are some choices. It's a bit like if you are thirsty and cold, which will you deal with first? Some will have a drink of water first and others may put on a sweater first. Mostly you don't think about which you do first, it just happens because you are largely unconscious of them. But when you are dating you need to know whether you have enough between you to sustain a significant relationship, which means you need to make your values a little more conscious and see what the fit is with his.

If you absolutely must have passion but don't care if he has a university degree, then it's important to know that. If he is highly intellectual but cannot talk to you about intimate and relationship matters, then the likelihood of you having a fulfilling long term relationship are slim indeed. My man must have honour and integrity if he is to win and keep me: they are my No. 1 values, followed closely by emotional availability, purpose and intelligence. I would also adore him to be spiritually conscious but he doesn't have to be in the same carriage as me, just on the same train and heading in the same direction.

Now I know we'd all love a tall dark handsome man, or maybe a blond blue eyed Adonis, but what they look like is not who they are. Who they are is determined by their values and much more important than looks. In my workshops it often takes participants ages to work out what they want in a relationship and when they do, it sometimes surprises them.

Whilst your and his values don't all need to be the same, and of course they never will be, if say you valued certainty and he valued adventure really high, you might have a clash in lifestyle that would make a permanent relationship challenging. You'd want to be saving for the mortgage, and he'd want to be jumping out of planes or climbing mountains: maybe not a keeper.

You need to value some of the same top things to be great friends and to form the basis for a relationship. And you need the differences too because they will create more passion. You must know what yours are, and what you can't and won't move, and you must know what he values and what he can't and won't move. You know you can't change someone's nature and while what he eats and what he wears and stuff like that can be modified down the track it's unlikely his core values will change much except with unusual circumstances such as illness or financial hardship or a family crisis. So don't worry if he's not in Armani jeans on the first date, you must focus on who he is in his heart and what he wants in a relationship and how his core values influence his life. They are what matter and they are the basis for a great relationship that is passionate and lasting.

So how do you find out what his values are on the first date? You ask questions. You ask him what he loves doing; how he spends his leisure time. You ask him whether he loves his job or career. You ask him what he thinks about most. You ask him what he is most passionate about. You ask him where he would like to be in 10, 20, 30 years, depending on his age. You ask him about his relationships with his parents, his siblings or his kids. You ask him what he's done in life that he is most proud of. And there are a million other questions you can ask, all of which will tell you what he values.

To him they are just questions you are asking to get to know him. He probably won't have a clue that you are taking note of the answers to determine whether he could be a keeper. But it will give you a huge amount of information so that you are not just going on whether he is visually pleasing or you feel some chemistry between you. You are actually gathering real intelligence as to whether you should date him again.

Sally, 39, an accountant, met Mike, a semi-retired lawyer for lunch one day. He seemed pleasant, was certainly intelligent, clearly he was financially well off and he liked to travel; all of which she loved and absolutely wanted in her next relationship. But the downside was his decision to play golf 4 days a week whilst she was building her business and wanting to work for many more years. It could have worked, if they had worked at it, but she just didn't see herself as a golfing widow at weekends. Sally wanted someone who was still passionate about his career and was intellectually stimulated by what he did every day.

Even before you meet you can ask these kinds of questions, or get some idea from a man's profile. Jessica, 27, a hair stylist, was being hounded by a rather gorgeous looking man on the internet who was divorced with two young children. She was clear on her profile that she wanted a single man without children and despite his good looks and all the other things they appeared to have in common it was a real values issue for her and she chose not to meet with him. When Lucy met Steve she wanted to have kids but he had two already and was not keen. They spent three years together and nothing changed except her diminishing child bearing age so she left him and went on to meet Matthew and had 2 gorgeous kids with him.

> **Know that the risk of not loving is greater than the risk of loving. Dr Buzz McCarthy**

So you can determine whether your date, Mr Right Now, can turn into Mr Right by getting a handle on his values, seeing if they fit against your own and deciding consciously whether to make the first date the last date, or whether to agree to a second date. This is not rocket science: it is asking the right questions and listening to the answers and evaluating all the information to see if you could live with this man. Then you are taking the emphasis off his looks, his bank balance and the chemistry: all of which can change tomorrow or in a decade. What he values is his choice; what you value is yours. Whether your values and his values are truly compatible for a long term relationship is your choice. Make it wisely and make it soon. If they are not, move on. Remember the universe has a back-up plan. If he is not Mr Right, you may want to keep him around for a while as Mr Right Now or you may want to move on. Choose wisely. Do not do it like a dating addict who needs perfection in everything, know you are both flawed. Just look at his flaws

171

against his values, look at your flaws against your values and you will know whether this man is the perfect match for you or not.

NOTE TO SELF

♥ **I know what I value most in life and in my intimate relationships**

♥ **I will get to know what he values to see if there is a good match**

♥ **I will never give up on my dreams**

CHAPTER TWENTY

SEX - WHEN AND WHEN NOT

There are websites whose sole purpose is to help people get laid. No pretence, no hiding behind legitimacy, and no absence of photos or lists of desires. If that is what you want, go for it. But they are not for the women who sincerely want a committed and loving relationship with a genuine guy. Sadly, the lines are blurred and lots of men go on genuine dating sites simply to find sex. Why, I'm not sure; it's like if you want tennis shoes you don't look in the bra section of the store, you go direct to the shoes. And since there are enough sites to get sex I wish they would stick to them but they don't.

It reminds me of a time when I was working for a secretarial agency based at the London Hilton Hotel. Its aim was to provide office services for visiting executives in the days before laptops and the internet. So night after night I would sit typing a shipping contract or a play for some visiting Japanese or American and hopefully go away with a nice tip for working through the night. One night I was called to Claridges to work for a Persian executive who greeted me at the door in his dressing gown and a bottle of Scotch in his hand. Immediately on guard I sat with my portable typewriter on my knee and asked him about his work. Suggesting we should have a drink before we started work he poured me a Scotch and opened a giant bag of pistachio nuts fresh from Persia. Of course there was no work and it became clear he had other things on his mind. So I stood up, thanked him for the drink and told him he had clearly rung the wrong agency and that there were many other outlets in London for what he wanted. And I left. This is exactly what I suggest every good woman does when she is inappropriately contacted via a dating site and she knows he only wants sex.

So you've been through the preliminaries of a new internet contact, you find a new man to meet and you go hoping it will be nice to get to know him. He'll be there hoping it will lead to sex. He'll ask you leading questions to ascertain if you are interested and usually he's very skilled at this. Whether you're interested or not, this is not the time to agree to sex. On your first dates you should be finding out what his values are, what he makes important in life, and assessing whether he is the sort of man you want to be in relationship with, not deciding on sex. You must not be drawn into conversation that makes you feel uncomfortable or uneasy or pressured to have sex with him. Ladies, it is your job, not his, to decide on the time for sex: always. Don't make the mistake of thinking you won't see him again unless you have sex, for the opposite is more likely to be the truth. If you have sex with him too early you may never have the opportunity to create a real relationship with him: chances are he may never ring you again, or he may only ring when he wants more easy sex and he thinks you'll oblige. And he'll disappear if you don't.

Ladies, what you need to know is that men actually feel cheated of a challenge when you come over too soon. Men in their masculine energy are all about focus, challenge, projects, strategies, results. It's what they do at work all day. They have an outcome, they look at the ways to get there and they look at cost effectiveness, time delay, team work and what they have to put in to get the job done. Having sex with you is no different. It's a project and there are certain things that he needs to do in order for it to really work for him. Starting with a casual physical relationship will never end up as something more meaningful and long term; it is not the way they work.

Whilst you probably have woken up feeling sad and sorry for yourself when you've had sex with a man who's name you hardly know and whose values you certainly don't, men tell me they feel exactly the same. They feel cheated. They feel flat and even sad. Just like you! And they feel that because you did not, in your easy agreement for too-early sex, allow them to do their job. You took their strategies away. You took their anticipation away. Men love the anticipation of having sex and if they really want you they will wait. For him that waiting and anticipating is the real thrill so when you give in too soon you actually deprive him of something very important to him in the mating game. Of course they enjoy instant sex too, but men like a girl who has standards and they are more likely to pursue her if she says no for a while.

Men are hunters and ladies want to be hunted. Every woman I know wants a man to pursue her. And yet these days' women do all the pursuing... they instigate text messages, emails and phone calls and they ask men for dates and for sex. Ladies, you should do absolutely none of these in the early days of a relationship otherwise how will you know if he really cares? Just as you enjoy the feminine role of being pursued, he enjoys his masculine role of hunting and anticipating. So relax into your feminine energy and enjoy the pursuit. Do none of the communicating and allow yourself the luxury of deciding when the relationship feels OK enough for you to feel safe having sex.

> **Life without love is like a tree without blossoms or fruit.**
> **Khalil Gibran**

Let him wait for sex. He may be spoiled by all the other women who have had sex with him on a first date but that is of no consequence to you. You are different, you have standards and that means you may have to exercise some self-restraint too. You have to wait too, even if you want it. Even if you haven't had it for ages. You can wait and you must if you want to find a really good man for a long term committed relationship. Then when you decide sex is OK you should have a feeling for his values and for his level of interest in you beyond the bedroom. If he's stuck around for a few dates and invested a good amount of time in getting to know you without sex, he's worth looking at for a real relationship.

So if you're feeling good about this man and you feel you are getting to know him, talk about sex beforehand. If you have standards and care about yourself, you need to know he's not having sex with other women. You need to know that he's interested in you otherwise it may well be great sex, but fleeting and you'll wonder what happened and why you feel awful when you don't hear from him again. You need to know he'll call you the next day and make plans to see you again. And you need to have a conversation with him about taking your profiles off-line and not being available to other partners. Otherwise you're not exclusive and you still don't know him well enough to know he's not flirting with other women and wanting to meet other internet dates and nor does he know that about you.

Remember that if you decide to say no at any stage, that's your right. If he vanishes into the woodwork, let him go. You won't get him back for any length of time because you're good at sex, he will come back because he likes you and because you have standards.

If you are in the pre-dating stage and he comes on too quickly or too strong, or his sexual advances make you feel uncomfortable, you should end the conversation and delete him from your on-line mail box. And if he does it when you meet you have the right to excuse yourself and leave.

Sex is wonderful and it needs to be safe, loving, fun and with someone you can trust. Ladies use your intuition and make sure before you get sexually involved that this man is prepared to offer you a relationship. If he's not, move on and find someone who is. It's all about your standards, and when you find Mr Right, you'll be pleased you had those standards which led to a loving and committed relationship.

NOTE TO SELF

♥ **Giving in before I want will not keep him at my door**

♥ **I will wait for sex until I am ready**

♥ **I will ask for exclusivity first**

CHAPTER TWENTY-ONE

MR RIGHT

How quickly you meet and connect with Mr Right is probably up to you. He is out there. He's in the supermarket queue; he's on the tennis court, in the library, at the office and on the internet.

Your willingness and openness to be in a relationship is the first key. You have to decide you want to have a partner, commit to dating (even if you think you will meet "Him" on a plane or in a disco), know what you want and what you don't want and be prepared to be vulnerable.

You'll create your internet dating profile, and you'll create your standards and you'll open your heart and you'll wait. You'll take your three-piece business suit off at the end of the day and forget about running a business, or whatever you do for a living or a career. Men need to feel they have something to offer you. If you are so competent at everything you do they don't know how they can add to your life and they'll go to another woman whom they feel has a place for them.

> **Vulnerability is our greatest gift and our greatest strength.**
> **Dr Buzz McCarthy**

Vulnerability is our greatest gift and our greatest strength. It is what opens our hearts to someone enough that we can actually feel what is going on instead of doing all our feeling through our brain. It doesn't mean being stupid or having a blonde moment; it just means allowing yourself to feel your way into a relationship with your heart and allowing a space for someone to offer you something. Men also need to know you are interested in them.... they want to feel a connection with you or else they will move on, so when you are with him, if you are interested, he needs to know that. Not by what you say but by what he feels. That means engaging with him and opening your heart fully. It's not easy, ladies tell me, it's a scary place if you let it, but what is the alternative? It's staying home alone for the rest of your life with your cat and your bottle of red and never fully loving in a relationship that will alternatively make your heart sing and make you cry, it will make you angry, furious and deliriously happy. There'll be times when you'll want to throw stuff, drown your cat and your sorrows and you will drink all the red! But it will make you feel alive....and that's a huge upside on how most people feel these days, which is half dead.

So go out and find your Mr Right and don't settle for Mr Right Now.

> **The most beautiful things in the world cannot be seen or heard. They must be felt by the heart.** **Helen Keller**

Make sure you are emotionally available when you set out on the journey; know you want a committed relationship but don't be desperate. Know that you need to give and give and give and that he won't be perfect. And be prepared to love again even if you've been hurt. The past does not equal the future so get on and create a new future with this Mr Right.

How he treats you is all up to you and the standards you set. You have to create the flavour of the relationship; that's your job, so start it the way you want to proceed.

Everything he asks you from the beginning will be to ascertain your standards, although he probably doesn't know that. Especially about sex. Don't get caught up in his stuff about sex too soon if that doesn't work for you. If he really wants you, he'll wait. And if you come across too soon, he'll be happy in the moment but he won't respect you and he'll move on.

He'll know if you conduct yourself with integrity and if that's what he wants he'll hang around. So you'll know if he continues to contact you and wants to see you he's interested.

181

That's why you let him do all the communication in the early days. If you did all the doing, how would you know if he was really interested, or whether he was just filling in time and waiting for Ms Right to appear? You wouldn't.

Mr Right has a real life. He has interests and healthy activities he enjoys. He is not a lone wolf; he has friends he wants to hang out with. He has a job and earns money to create a life with.   He enjoys company and socialising and he's appreciative of family life.

He has a life away from the internet. He knows his role as the hunter; he's grown up to be a man that faces challenges head on. He'll do what he can to get a lot of sex but if it comes too easily he too will feel flat and empty afterwards. Just like you do when you have sex with someone where there is no heart connection.

He has good values and knows what's important in life. He'll conduct himself with integrity and will treat those around him honourably. And he doesn't want multiple women: he just wants one who shows she is interested in him.

To witness the life of someone you truly love is a rare gift.
Dr Buzz McCarthy

So how will you know him? Certainly I hope you will feel it. Not too many years ago we women used to be burnt alive at the stake for our intuition, so let's bring it out again and use it to determine if this one is capable of being our Mr Right.

He'll certainly be known by the amount of non-sexual time he is prepared to put in to get you.

He'll take you out and put some thought into what you two do together. He won't be the "got any plans?" type of man; he'll be booking you up days in advance so you can't accept another invitation from someone else for the weekend. He'll call you on the phone rather than have a sms relationship with you and he'll want to meet your friends and your family once he knows he's interested in you.

He'll ask about you; what you like, what your dreams are, what your life has been about and what you want it to be about, and you will ask him the same questions. He'll tell you first how he feels about you and he'll tell you he's gone off line because he wants to pursue an exclusive relationship with you.

One day, if the gods are smiling, he'll look into your eyes and see right into your soul and he'll decide he wants to have you forever.

183

Always remember how you play this game is up to you. You set the scene, you create the standards and you must always love yourself just a little bit more than you love him. Even when he's Mr Right, or specially when he's Mr Right.

NOTE TO SELF

♥   **I am committed to a long term passionate relationship with Mr Right**

♥   **I will be all that I can and give all that is me to this man when we commit**

♥   **I really want my relationship to be admired and respected by others**

CHAPTER TWENTY-TWO

THE FINAL WORD

Nothing in life is as beautiful as a loving and committed relationship with someone who fills your soul; a partner who is your raving fan and for whom you would walk over hot coals. It does happen and it can happen for you.

Whilst the mandate of every relationship is about giving love, it is also about what you are to learn so your intimate partner will also be your most profound teacher. Being open to what he or she can teach you is the ultimate gift you will give to both yourself and the relationship.

Decide to love and to let fear go: they cannot co-exist. If you are fearful you will attract more fear. If you are loving, you will attract more love. It's that simple.

Having clarity about what is really important for you in a relationship is vital and remember he will not be everything you want but he will be everything you need. Going for Mr Right should be your goal: I see too many people who have settled and are apathetic about much of their life because their soul no longer shines brightly. If you are with Mr Right Now and he does not meet the wildest dreams of the man you want to marry and spend the rest of your life with, if he is not educated highly enough, doesn't have enough money, had challenged relationships with his ex or his kids or his mum, if he doesn't share your lifestyle or whatever, he may still be your Mr Right. Only time and your heart will tell you. So listen, be in peace whilst you listen to the inner wisdom of your soul and decide whether you are going to love this man no matter what. And if you are, then celebrate wildly, and if you are not, then honour what you have had, let him go with grace and move on to what the gods have next in store for you. And always go with gratitude for everyone with whom you are in an intimate relationship with has been a gift for you, even when you can't see it right then and remember that each end is always a new beginning.

In love and in life, if you don't find a way to serve you will never be happy. **Dr Buzz McCarthy**

NOTE TO SELF

♥　　**I love without fear**

♥　　**I am open to learning from my Mr Right**

♥　　**I am excited that I know now how to be different in intimate relationships**

186

ABOUT THE AUTHOR

DR BUZZ McCARTHY

Buzz is a bestselling author and recognised as a leading specialist in the area of intimate relationships, wealth, success and personal transformation. She is passionate about helping people make more compelling choices and creating more passion and success in their lives.

Buzz has spent this time of Covid-19 high in the hills of Tuscany where the rarefied air and the changed circumstances of her life have propelled her to do her best ever work. She is coaching clients around the world in relationship and other matters.

For the past 4 decades Buzz has worked, travelled, consulted and spoken to hundreds of thousands of people in many countries who have wanted to empower their lives. For more than 25 years she has worked with one of the world's most prominent thought leaders as one of his elite trainers.

Buzz started her wealth creation at the age of 16, trading shares; a passion which led her to become self-sufficient at an early age and living a life that many would aspire to.

She has a Doctoral Degree in Psychoneurology and is a Member of the American Board of Psychoneurology. She divides her time between her Tuscan home, London and Australia.

Made in the USA
Monee, IL
20 January 2022